STAYING

PUT

STAYING PUT

PUT

MAKING
A HOME
IN A RESTLESS
WORLD

SCOTT RUSSELL SANDERS

BEACON PRESS

BOSTON

Beacon Press
25 Beacon Street
Boston, Massachusetts 02108-2892

Beacon Press books
are published under the auspices of
the Unitarian Universalist Association of Congregations.

99 98 97 96 95 94 93   8 7 6 5 4 3 2

Text design by Ruth Kolbert

The author and publisher gratefully acknowledge the following publications, in which earlier versions of chapters from this book first appeared:
"After the Flood" in *Townships*, ed. Michael Martone (Iowa City: University of Iowa Press, 1992); "House and Home" in *Notre Dame Magazine*; "Earth's Body" and "Ground Notes" in *The North American Review*;
"The Force of Moving Water" in *Always a River*, ed. Robert L. Reid
(Bloomington: Indiana University Press, 1991) and (under the title
"Looking at a River") in *The American Voice*; "Settling Down" (under the
title "Staying Put") and "Telling the Holy" in *Orion*; and "Wayland" in
The Gettysburg Review. Excerpt from "The Design of a House" from *Collected Poems, 1957–1982*, copyright © 1969, 1984 by Wendell Berry, pub-
lished by North Point Press and reprinted by permission of Farrar, Straus
& Giroux, Inc.; excerpt from "Roots" from *Henry's Fate* by John Berryman, copyright © 1977 by Kate Berryman, reprinted by permission of
Farrar, Straus & Giroux, Inc.

Library of Congress Cataloging-in-Publication Data

Sanders, Scott R. (Scott Russell), 1945–
Staying put : making a home in a restless world / Scott Russell
Sanders.
p.   cm. — (The Concord library)
Includes bibliographical references.
ISBN 0-8070-6340-1
I. Title. II. Series.
PS3569.A5137S7   1993
814'.54—dc20   92-35629
CIP

For DESSA *and* EARL MCCLURE,
who have shared their daughter with me,
and once again for that daughter,
this time and always,
RUTH

CONTENTS

WORDS OF THANKS

I can name here only a few of the many people who lit the path I followed in writing this book. The steadiest light has come from my wife, Ruth Ann McClure Sanders, from our children, Jesse and Eva, and from my mother, who is also Eva. They are my first and dearest reasons for staying put.

I could not understand the meaning of neighborhood without neighbors, and I have been blessed with fine ones; I am grateful to Malcolm Dalglish, Judy Klein, Alvin and Erna Rosenfeld, Roger Mitchell, Lara and Farough Abed, Michael Hamburger, and Jenny Bass, for the sharing of food, music, tools, work, and talk.

By their actions and letters and conversations, often in ways they may not have realized, friends

have taught me a great deal; I thank in particular
Lauren Bryant, Nicholas Delbanco, John Elder,
Robert Finch, John Gallman, Edward Hoagland,
Douglas Hofstadter, Charles Johnson, David Kline,
Ursula Le Guin, Phillip Lopate, Barry Lopez,
Michael Martone, Erin McGraw, William Nichols,
Tony Stoneburner, Brian Swann, James Alexander
Thom, Deanne Urmy, and Don Wallis.

Although this book celebrates the virtues of sitting
still, I did a fair amount of traveling while writing it.
I am grateful to the good people who opened their
homes to me: William and Martha Schafer, Judy and
Eric Homberger, Patrick and Gretchen McCaskey,
Deborah Galyan and Michael Wilkerson, Barbara and
Christer Mossberg, and above all Dick and Jane
Holden.

My colleagues at Indiana University and my
students, especially those in the course called
"Imagining Nature," have nourished me: to all of
them, without a long catalog of names, I give thanks.
Thomas Schorgl at the Indiana Arts Commission,
along with David Hoppe and Kenneth Gladish at the
Indiana Humanities Council, have encouraged and
supported my work in many ways. My deep thanks
to Aina Niemela, Parker Huber, Olivia and Marion
Gilliam, and others associated with *Orion* magazine,
for including me in their gatherings, and for their
work on behalf of the earth.

I tried out parts of this book as talks, and I wish to
thank the institutions as well as the people who
hosted me: Wayne Dodd at Ohio University; David
Anderson at Hiram College; John Elder at

Middlebury College; Peter Greer at Phillips Exeter Academy; Philip O'Connor at Bowling Green State University; William Nichols at Denison University; Rebecca Blair at Westminster College; Robert Grindy at Richland Community College; Barbara Mossberg at the University of Helsinki; and Stan Rubin at SUNY-Brockport.

Fellowships from the Indiana Arts Commission and the John Simon Guggenheim Memorial Foundation freed me from other duties so that I could work on this book, and I am grateful.

PREFACE

On coming to a new place, my father would take a pinch of dirt, sprinkle it in his palm, sniff it, stir it with a blunt finger, squeeze it, then rake it on his tongue, tasting. When I first saw him do this, I was puzzled. Why eat dirt? "Just trying to figure out where I am," he explained.

This book is my own tasting of the dirt, my effort to find out where I am. It records my attempt to fashion a life that is firmly grounded—in household and community, in knowledge of place, in awareness of nature, and in contact with that source from which all things rise. I aspire to become an inhabitant, one who knows and honors the land. In these pages I follow various and sometimes crooked paths, yet I am always driven by a single desire, that of learning

to be at home. The search is practical as well as
spiritual. Only by understanding where I live can I
learn how to live.

There's no need to go looking for home, of course,
unless you're lost. I have been lost, in ways no map
could remedy. I cannot return to my native ground
and take up residence there. The farm in Tennessee
where I spent my earliest years is buried under
asphalt; the military reservation where I lived next is
locked away behind fences and soldiers; and the farm
in Ohio where I spent the rest of my childhood has
been erased entirely, the house and barn bulldozed by
the army, the woods and fields flooded by a
boondoggle dam. If I am to have a home, it can only
be a place I have come to as an adult, a place I have
chosen.

The place I have chosen surrounds an old brick
house on a street of slow trees and quick children, in a
city named, so the story goes, for its fields of flowers.
The core of my territory is the area within walking
distance of my front door, a rolling, wooded,
potholed terrain known as karst landscape because it
is defined by the erosion of limestone; and that core is
encircled by the worn, unglaciated hills of southern
Indiana; and these hills bristling with beech, maple,
and oak, these creeks dappled with sycamores, these
flowering fields are embraced by the watershed of the
Ohio River.

What can be seen from my window, what can be
reached on foot within a day's walk of my house,
may seem tame enough: no surf breaks on rocky

shores, no mountains gleam with snow, no bears prowl. It is a settled region, marked everywhere by human presence. But for all our buildings and lights and roads, for all our signs and words, that human presence is only a thin film stretched over mystery. Let sunlight flame in a blade of grass, let night come on, let thunder roar and tornado whirl, let the earth quake, let muscles twitch, let mind curl about the least pebble or blossom or bird, and the true wildness of this place, of all places, reveals itself.

My nation's history does not encourage me, or anyone, to belong somewhere with a full heart. A vagabond wind has been blowing here for a long while, and it grows stronger by the hour. I feel the force of it, and brace my legs to keep from staggering. My father left his native Mississippi at age twenty and spent the rest of his years on the move, following the grain of marriage and money and jobs. He kept tasting the dirt in each new place because, after childhood, he never again had a settled home, never lived anywhere with the intention of staying.

I wish to consider the virtue and discipline of staying put. I dwell here in company—with my wife and children, my neighbors, the people of my city, and with all the creatures that run and root and soar. I desire no home apart from this companionship. Although I have lived in the same region, indeed the same house, for twenty years, I am still discovering what it means to be a citizen. I have lived in one marriage even longer, and yet I am still discovering what it means to be a husband and father. For me, the effort to be grounded in family and community is inseparable from the effort to be grounded in place.

I believe we can only be adequate to the earth if we are adequate to our neighborhoods. At the same time, we can live wisely in our chosen place only if we recognize its connections to the rest of the planet. The challenge is to see one's region as a focus of processes that extend over the earth and out to the edges of the universe; to realize that *this* place is only one of an infinite number of places where the powers of nature show forth.

Tracing even a few of these connections has required me to make an amateur's raid into the domains of experts, among them physicists, philosophers, folklorists, astronomers, biologists, anthropologists, and theologians. This may be foolhardy, but I make no apologies. We are all amateurs when it comes to understanding our place in the web of things. Nor do I apologize for trying to speak at once about the geography of land and the geography of spirit. They are one terrain.

The work of belonging to a place is never finished. There will always be more to know than any mind or lifetime can hold. But that is no argument against learning all one can. What I understand so far I have gathered into these narratives, which are bound together by the ancient plot of a journey into the wilderness in search of vision. The wilderness I seek is always underfoot, and the power I seek flows in with every breath. We cannot lay hold of the sacred; we can only point toward it, say where we have

glimpsed it. This book points through my local
ground to the shapely energies we call nature, and
through nature to the encompassing order for which
we have no adequate name.

S. R. S.
Bloomington, Indiana

We have failed to live up to our geography.
THEODORE ROETHKE

People usually consider walking on water
or in thin air a miracle.
But I think the real miracle
is not to walk either on water or in thin air,
but to walk on earth.
THICH NHAT HANH

CHAPTER ONE

AFTER THE FLOOD

ARIVER POURED THROUGH the landscape I knew as a child. It was the power of the place, gathering rain and snowmelt, surging through the valley under sun, under ice, under the bellies of fish and the curled brown boats of sycamore leaves. You will need a good map of Ohio to find the river I am talking about, the West Branch of the Mahoning. The stretch of it I knew best no longer shows on maps, a stretch that ran between wooded slopes and along the flanks of cornfields and pastures in the township of Charlestown, in Portage County, a rural enclave surrounded by the smokestacks and concrete of Akron, Youngstown, and Cleveland in the northeastern corner of the state.

Along that river bottom I gathered blackberries and

hickory nuts, trapped muskrats, rode horses, followed baying hounds on the scent of raccoons. Spring and fall, I walked barefoot over the tilled fields, alert for arrowheads. Along those slopes I helped a family of Swedish farmers collect buckets of maple sap. On the river itself I skated in winter and paddled in summer, I pawed through gravel bars in search of fossils, I watched hawks preen and pounce, I courted and canoed and idled. This remains for me a primal landscape, imprinted on my senses, a place by which I measure every other place.

It is also, now, a drowned landscape. In the early 1960s, when I was in high school, politicians and bankers and realtors ordained that the Mahoning should be snared. A dam was built, the river died, and water backed up over most of the land I knew. No city needed the water for drinking. The reservoir, named after a man who had never lived in that valley, provided owners of loud boats with another playground for racing and waterskiing, and provided me with a lesson in loss. If the loss were mine alone, the story would not be worth telling. My grieving for a drowned landscape is private, a small ache in a bruised world. But the building of the dam, the obliteration of that valley, the displacement of people and beasts, these were public acts, the sort of acts we have been repeating from coast to coast as we devour the continent.

Like many townships in farm country, remote from the offices where the fate of land is decided, Charlestown has suffered more than one erasure. Long before the building of the reservoir, the government had already sliced away the northern third of the township for an arsenal, a wild, murderous place I have written about elsewhere as a paradise of bombs. On current maps of the township that upper third is blank white, and most of the remaining two-thirds, flooded by the reservoir, is vacant blue. Merely by looking at the map, one can tell that here is a sacrificial zone.

Returning to one's native ground, always tricky, becomes downright treacherous when the ground is at the bottom of a lake. Unwilling to dive through so much water, I can return to that drowned landscape, as I can return to childhood, only by diving through memory.

I had just become a teenager when the government began purchasing the farms and trailers and shacks that would be in the path of the reservoir. (If there had been mansions and factories in the way, the politicians would have doomed a different valley.) Among the first to be unhoused was the Swedish family, old Mr. Sivvy and his two unmarried children, who had farmed that bottom land with big-shouldered horses, whose silage I had pitchforked in the steaming silo, whose cows I had fed, whose maple syrup I had savored hot from the vat. Uprooted, the old man soon died. The children bought a new farm on high ground, trying to start over, but it was no good, the soil too thin, worn out, no black bottom land, no fat maples, no river pouring through it. All down the valley it was the same, people forced to move by a blizzard of government paper, occasionally by the sheriff, in a few instances by the arrival of bulldozers at their front door.

While gangs of men with dynamite and dump trucks tore down the condemned buildings, other gangs with earthmovers and cement mixers slowly raised a wall across the river. For a year I watched it rise, while I wooed a girl who lived on a ridge over-looking the dam site. Crooners purred love songs from the stereo in her parlor, against an accompaniment of chuffs and shouts and whistles from the valley below. I studied the contours of that girl's face while the river's contours were bullied into the shape of blueprints. The huge concrete forms, the tinkertoy scaffolds, the blasting, the snort of compressors, the lurch of heavy machines are confused in me now with the memory of damp hands and lingering kisses. The girl and I broke up, but the concrete held. Thereafter, I avoided that ridge, and did not see the laying of the dam's final tier, did not see the steel gates close. By the time I graduated from high school, water was beginning to lap over the banks of the Mahoning, but I could not bear to go down to the river and look.

When I left Ohio for college, my family left as well, trailing my father's work to Louisiana. My childhood friends dispersed—to war, to jail, to distant marriages and jobs, to cities where lights glittered and dollars sang. I had scant reason to visit that flooded township and good reason to keep my distance. Why rush to see a muddy expanse of annihilating water?

Some years later, however, duties carried me through the northeastern corner of Ohio, within an hour's drive of my old neighborhood. I had not planned to make a detour. Yet the names of towns emblazoned on huge green signs along the highway tugged at me. The shapes of chimneys and roofs, the colors of barns, the accents in fast-food booths and gas stations, all drew me off the interstate onto the roads of Portage County, up the stream of recollection toward that childhood place.

The season of my return was late winter, after the last snow and before the first plowing, before grass resumed its green sizzle, before trees blurred with leaves. The shape of the land lay exposed. It was a gray day, a day to immunize one against nostalgia, a day safe, I supposed, for facing up to what I had lost. Surely I was prepared by now to see the great erasure. I was a man, and had put behind me a boy's affection for a stretch of river and a patch of dirt. New places had claimed me, thereby loosening the grip of that old landscape. Still, to ease my way back, before going to the reservoir I drove through the county seat, Ravenna, which had scarcely changed, and then through Edinburgh, Atwater, Deerfield, Palmyra, Paris, Wayland—tiny crossroad settlements where I had played baseball and eaten pie and danced—and these, too, had scarcely changed. Circling, I drew closer and closer to the blue splotch on the map.

The best way to approach the water, I decided, was along the road where, for half our years in Charlestown, my family had lived on five acres with horses and rabbits and dogs. Surely our gray-shingled house would still be there, safe on its ridge above the lake, even if most of the land I had known was drowned. So I turned from the highway onto that curving, cracked, tar-slick road, looking for the familiar. But at the corner, where there should have been a farmhouse, a silo, a barn, there was only a billboard marking the entrance to the West Branch Reservation. The fields where I had baled hay now bristled with a young woods. There was no house in the hollow where the road dipped down, where the family of Seventh Day Adventists used to live with their stacks of apocalyptic pamphlets and their sad-eyed children. The spinster's white bungalow was gone, along with the battered bus in the side yard which had served her for a chicken coop. Yard after yard had grown up in brush, and the shade trees spread darkness over their own seedlings. No mail boxes leaned on posts beside the road, no driveways broke the fringe of weeds. The trailer park was gone, the haunted house was gone, the tar-paper shanty where the drunk mechanic beat his wife and the wife beat her kids and the kids wailed, that was gone, and so was every last trailer and cottage and privy and shack, all down the blacktopped mile to our place.

I recognized our place by the two weeping willows out front. My father and I had planted those willows from slips, had fenced them round to protect the tender bark from deer, had watered and weeded and nursed them along. By the day of my visit those twigs had burgeoned into yellow fountains some fifty feet high, brimming over the woods that used to be our cleared land, woods that flourished where our house and barn had stood. I did not get out of the car. I could see from the road all that I was ready to see. The dense thicket, bare of leaves, was the color of rusty iron. Aside from the willows, no hint of our work or ownership survived.

I felt a fool. During the years of my absence, while my mind had suffered the waters to rise through the forest and up the ravines onto the margins of our land, I had preserved the gray-shingled house, the low white barn, the lilacs and forsythia, the orchard and pasture, the garden, the lawn. And yet, all the while, cedar and sumac and brambles, like the earth's dark fur, had been pushing up through my past.

Sight of the reservoir, surely, could not be worse. I continued down the road through the vigorous woods. Not a house, not a barn, not a plowed field. The first clearing I came to was half a mile farther on, at the spot where a man named Ferry had lived. He used to let the neighborhood kids swim in his pond, even after a boastful boy dived into a rock and drowned. We knew that when we knocked at Mr. Ferry's door, raising money for school or scouts, he would buy whatever we had to sell. He was a tender man. He loved his wife so much that when she died he planted a thousand white pines in her memory. The pines, spindly in my recollection, had grown into a forest by the day of my return.

In place of Mr. Ferry's house and yard there was a state campground now, encircled by the spiky green palisade of pines. The entrance booth was boarded up. A placard outside instructed campers to deposit their fees—so much for trailers, so much for tents—in the box below. There was no box below, only a slab of plywood with ragged holes from which the screws had been ripped. Nor were there any campers on this wintry afternoon. As I drove through the vacant lot, the only sounds were the crunch of gravel beneath my tires and the yawp of blue jays overhead and the shoosh of wind through the pines.

I pulled away from the campground and drove on. My mind raced ahead along the road as I remembered it, steeply downhill between fat maples and patchy sycamores to the river and the steel-girdered bridge. I had rolled down that hill in a school bus, swayed down on horseback, hurtled down on bicycle and sled, run down on foot. The slope and feel of it, fixed inside me, became my standard for all hills. From the bridge I had watched the river's current raveling over sandbars, minnows flickering in the shallows, water-striders dimpling the surface. Now and again, when the sun was right, I had spied my own face peering up from the stream. In memory, the road stretched on beyond the bridge, passing the tin-roofed shed where the maple syrup boiled, passing the Sivvy farm, rising up the far slope to a T-junction with a ridgeline road. Turn left from there, and I would go to the high school. Turn right, and I would go to the barbershop and feed store. As my thoughts raced ahead of the car, inside me the valley opened and the river flexed its long sleek muscle.

Rounding the curve, however, I had to slam on the brakes to avoid running into a guardrail that blocked the road. Beyond the railing, where valley and bridge and river should have been, flat gray water spread away toward distant hills. You know this moment from dream: You are in a familiar room, but when you turn to leave, where a door should be there is a wall; or you come up behind someone you love, speak her name, yet when she turns around her face is blank; or you find the story of the universe written on a page, but when you draw close to read it, the letters dissolve. Waters of separation, waters of oblivion, waters of death.

I got out of the car and pressed my thighs against the cold steel barricade and stared. Gray, flat, empty lake. Not even a boat to redeem the emptiness. A lone crow slowly pumped toward the horizon on glossy black wings. Along the shore, a few sycamores still thrust up their mottled branches. Except for those trees, the pavement beneath my boots, and hills too high for water to claim, everything I knew had been swept away.

My worst imaginings had failed to prepare me for this. I stood there dazed. I could not take it in, so much had been taken away. For a long spell I leaned against the guardrail and dredged up everything I could remember of what lay beneath the reservoir. But memory was at last defeated by the blank gray water. No effort of mind could restore the river or drain the valley. I surrendered to what my eyes were telling me. Only then was I truly exiled.

Those who built the dam had their reasons. You have heard the litany: flood control, recreation, development. I very much doubt that more human good has come from that muddy, silting, rarely frequented lake than came from the cultivated valley and wild woods and free-flowing river. I am suspicious of the logic that would forestall occasional floods by creating a permanent one. But I do not wish to debate the merits of dams. I mean only to speak of how casually, how relentlessly we sever the bonds between person and place.

One's native ground is the place where, since before you had words for such knowledge, you have known the smells, the seasons, the birds and beasts, the human voices, the houses, the ways of working, the lay of the land, and the quality of light. It is the landscape you learn before you retreat inside the illusion of your skin. You may love the place if you flourished there, or hate the place if you suffered there. But love it or hate it, you cannot shake free. Even if you move to the antipodes, even if you become intimate with new landscapes, you still bear the impression of that first ground.

I am all the more committed to know and care for the place I have come to as an adult because I have lost irretrievably the childhood landscapes that gave shape to my love of the earth. The farm outside Memphis where I was born has vanished beneath parking lots and the poison-perfect lawns of suburbs. The arsenal, with its herds of deer grazing on the grassy roofs of ammunition bunkers, is locked away behind chain-link fences, barbed wire, and guns. And the Mahoning Valley has been drowned. In our century, in our country, no fate could be more ordinary.

Of course, in mourning the drowned valley I also mourn my drowned childhood. The dry land preserved the traces of my comings and goings, the river carried the reflection of my beardless face. Yet even as a boy I knew that landscape was incomparably older than I, and richer, and finer. Some of the trees along the Mahoning had been rooted there when the first white settlers arrived from New England. Hawks had been hunting and deer had been drinking there since before our kind harnessed oxen. The gravels, laden with fossils, had been shoved there ten thousand years ago by glaciers. The river itself was the offspring of glaciers, a channel for meltwater to follow toward the Ohio, and thence to the Mississippi and the Gulf of Mexico. What I knew of the land's own history made me see that expanse of water as a wound.

Loyalty to place arises from sources deeper than narcissism. It arises from our need to be at home on the earth. We marry ourselves to the creation by knowing and cherishing a particular place, just as we join ourselves to the human family by marrying a particular man or woman. If the marriage is deep, divorce is painful. My drive down that unpeopled road and my desolate watch beside the reservoir gave me a hint of what others must feel when they are wrenched from their place. I say a *hint* because my loss is mild compared to what others have lost.

I think of the farmers who saw their wood lots and fields go under the flood. I think of the Miami and Shawnee who spoke of belonging to that land as a child belongs to a mother, and who were driven out by white soldiers. I think of the hundred other tribes that were herded onto reservations far from the graves of their ancestors. I think of the Africans who were yanked from their homes and bound in chains and shipped to this New World. I think about refugees, set in motion by hunger or tyranny or war. I think about children pushed onto the streets by cruelty or indifference. I think about migrant workers, dust bowl émigrés, all the homeless wanderers. I think about the poor everywhere—and it is overwhelmingly the poor—whose land is gobbled by strip mines, whose neighborhoods are wiped out by highways and shopping malls, whose villages are destroyed by bombs, whose forests are despoiled by chain saws and executive fountain pens.

The word *nostalgia* was coined in 1688 as a medical term, to provide an equivalent for the German word meaning homesickness. We commonly treat homesickness as an ailment of childhood, like mumps or chickenpox, and we treat nostalgia as an affliction of age. On our lips, nostalgia usually means a sentimental regard for the trinkets and fashions of an earlier time, for an idealized past, for a vanished youth. We speak of a nostalgia for the movies of the 1930s, say, or the haircuts of the 1950s. It is a shallow use of the word. The two Greek roots of *nostalgia* literally mean *return pain*. The pain comes not from returning home but from longing to return. Perhaps it is inevitable that a nation of immigrants—who shoved aside the native tribes of this continent, who enslaved and transported Africans, who still celebrate motion as if humans were dust motes—that such a nation should lose the deeper meaning of this word. A footloose people, we find it difficult to honor the lifelong, bone-deep attachment to place. We are slow to acknowledge the pain in yearning for one's native ground, the deep anguish in not being able, ever, to return.

On a warmer day I might have taken off my clothes and stepped over the guardrail and waded on down that road under the lake. Where the water was too deep, I could have continued in a boat, letting down a line to plumb the bottom. I would not be angling for death, which is far too easy to catch, but for life. To touch the ground even through a length of rope would be some consolation. The day was cold, however, and I was far from anyone who knew my face. So I climbed into the car and turned away and drove back through the resurgent woods.

CHAPTER TWO

HOUSE
AND
HOME

W HEN OUR FIRST CHILD
was born, a rosy wriggle of a girl we named Eva, my
wife and I were living in a second-floor apartment on
the noisiest avenue leading east and west through
Bloomington, Indiana. Trucks grinding their gears,
belching buses, howling ambulances and squad cars,
unmufflered pickups and juiced-up jalopies roared past
our windows, morning, noon, and night. What little
dirt we could find between pavement and weeds in our
tiny yard was slimed with engine oil.

To begin with, Eva weighed only six-and-a-half
pounds, all of them fidgety. Like any newborn she was
pure appetite. With a stomach so small, she hardly
seemed to close her eyes between feedings. Even when
those brown eyes did fitfully close, they would snap

open again at the least sound. Ruth nursed her to sleep, or I rocked her to sleep, and we'd lay her in the crib as gingerly as a bomb. Then some loud machine would come blaring down the street, and Eva would twitch and wail.

Once an engine had frightened her, mere milk would not soothe this child, nor would a cradle endlessly rocking. Only songs would do, a rivery murmur while she snuggled against a warm chest, and the chest had to be swaying in rhythm to a steady walk. Fall silent or stop moving and you had a ruckus on your hands. Night after night, I worked my way through *The Folk Songs of North America*, cover to cover and back again, while carrying Eva in circles over the crickety floorboards. It took hours of singing and miles of walking to lull her to stillness in my arms, and then a siren or diesel could undo the spell in seconds.

After seven nearly sleepless months, Ruth and I exchanged bleary stares over the breakfast table one morning and muttered, as in a single breath, "We've got to move."

That day we set out looking for a house. Not just any house, but the right one, the inevitable one, the one made in carpenter's heaven to fit our family. But how to find this perfect place among the countless ones available? Even allowing for the fact that we had no money to speak of, there were still hundreds of possibilities. How to choose? It was a problem as difficult, and nearly as consequential, as finding a mate to marry.

To compound the difficulty, Ruth and I carried in our heads quite different postcards of the ideal house, for she had grown up in a city and I had grown up in the country. She wanted a sturdy old box shaded by sturdy old trees, within a few steps of the place next door, in a neighborhood of sidewalks and flower beds where folks traded recipes and sat on their porches and pushed babies in buggies at dusk. I wanted a log cabin beside a pond in three hundred acres of woods bordering on a wilderness. Failing that, I would settle for a run-down farmhouse on a dirt road unknown to maps.

We compromised by buying a house in town that was as badly in need of repair as any cabin in the country. Five lines in the For Sale by Owner section of the newspaper led us there:

> CHARMING 2-story brick, walk
> to work, Bryan Park & Elm
> Heights. 3 bedrms., bath, liv.
> rm. with fireplace. 1113 East
> Wylie. $25,000.

Now that was cheap, even in 1974—not so cheap that I ever supposed we would live long enough to pay it off; nor so cheap that the loan officers at Workingmen's Federal didn't stare at us hard with their fiduciary gaze—but still, we could cover a monthly note on $25,000 without going naked or hungry.

More alluring than the price, however, was the location. That section of Wylie proved to be a two-block sanctuary of silence, cut off at one end by a cross-street, at the other end by woods. No trucks, no sirens, no hustling jalopies. You could hear birds in the big trees, crickets in the grass, children on screened porches. At night, in the hush of a bedroom, you could hear a baby breathe. The houses were old and sturdy enough to please Ruth; the park just around the corner gave me a taste of country, with its green swells, sunsets, and star-spangled skies.

We had already toured more houses than Washington slept in before we set our hearts on 1113 East Wylie. Whether it was charming, as the ad promised, the eye of the beholder would have to decide; but no one could doubt that it needed work. Realtors, in their cheery lingo, would have called it a fixer-upper or a handyman's dream. On our initial visit we made a list of items that would require swift attention, from roof to foundation. Of course we'd patch up that plaster, Ruth and I assured one another. We'd tear out that threadbare carpet and refinish the floors. We'd mend the chimney, ventilate the attic, dry up the basement, enclose the front porch, hang new doors, make over the kitchen, patch and paint and seal.

We moved in almost twenty years ago, and we are still working on that list. The list, in fact, has grown, season by season, like adult grief or the national debt. For every job completed, two new jobs arise. Reglaze a broken window, and before you've put away your tools a gutter sags or a switch burns out. In an old house, when handyman or handywoman takes on entropy, entropy always wins. Things fall apart—and not only in politics and religion. Pipes rust, nails work loose, shingles crumble, wood warps. The smooth turns rough and the straight grows crooked. A house is a shell caught in a surf that never stops grinding.

Over those same twenty years, our girl grew up. No longer a light sleeper, Eva went off to college last fall, having lived up to every beautiful promise in those original six-and-a-half pounds. The vague bundle of possibilities that lay in the crib, suckled on milk and swaddled in song, has become a definite person. How to explain the continuity from baby to young woman, when every molecule in her body has been replaced and her mind has filled up with the world?

Unable to answer that, and more than a little blue about Eva's going away, I work on the house and consider how it holds me. Of course there is no single right place to live, any more than there is a single right man or woman to marry. And yet, having made my choice, I feel wedded to this house, as I do to my wife and my neighborhood and my region. To become attached to a woman, sure, and to neighbors, fair enough, and maybe even to the local terrain—but to a pile of brick and wood? How has this box, this frame of possibilities, come to fit me so exactly? By what alchemy does a house become a home?

The short answer is that these walls and floors and scruffy flower beds are saturated with our memories and sweat. Everywhere I look I see the imprint of hands, everywhere I turn I hear the babble of voices, I smell sawdust or bread, I recall bruises and laughter. After nearly two decades of intimacy, the house dwells in us as surely as we dwell in the house.

By American standards it's small, plain, old-fashioned: a cube roughly twenty-five feet on a side, encased in yellow brick, with a low porch across the front, a wet basement below, and on top a roof in the shape of a pyramid. I have touched every one of those bricks, scraping ivy or pointing up the joints with fresh mortar. I have banged every joist and rafter, brushed every foundation stone. I know its crooks and crannies, its faults and fillings, as well as my dentist knows my teeth.

I could blame or thank my father and mother for the itch that keeps me tinkering. During my childhood, they fixed up their own series of dilapidated houses, turning sows' ears into silk purses, thereby convincing me that a place isn't truly yours until you rebuild it with your own hands. Thoreau, who cobbled together the most famous cabin in our literature, complained in *Walden* that "I never in all my walks came across a man engaged in so simple and natural an occupation as building his house." Had he been a contemporary of my father or me, he could have walked by our doors most weekends and found us hammering.

A month after we moved in, my parents came from Oklahoma to inspect the house and dandle Eva. As soon as my father could bear to put the baby down, he walked to the basement and opened the fuse box, hummed darkly, then came back upstairs and removed the faceplate from a light switch and peered inside. Turning to me with a frown, he said, "Son, you've got to rewire this house. I won't have my granddaughter sleeping in a firetrap."

"I've been meaning to get to that," I told him.

"We'll get to it starting this afternoon," he said. "Now where would you buy electrical supplies?"

We did start that afternoon, and Ruth and I kept on for months after my parents had gone back to Oklahoma. Room by room, we replaced every outlet, every switch, every wire, fishing new three-strand cable down from the attic or up from the basement, driving copper stakes into the soil to drain away any loose amps, until the juice from Public Service Indiana flowed innocuously.

During their visit the following winter, my father ran his hands over the walls in Eva's room. More dark humming. He lit a match, blew it out, then held the smoking stub near the window beside her crib. I knew what was coming. "Son," he announced, "you've got to insulate and weatherstrip and caulk, or my baby's going to catch pneumonia."

That job took two years, because Ruth and I decided not just to dribble loose fill into the wall cavities but to rip them open and do it right, with fiberglass batts and polyethylene vapor barrier and new sheetrock. Eva slept in our room while we tore hers apart. When I pried away the lath and plaster next to where her crib had stood, I found a message scrawled in carpenter's chalk on the pine sheathing: BILLY WALES IS A STINKER! JUNE 12, 1926. The taunt was so mild, I thought about leaving that part of the cavity exposed, with a frame around it; but that would have allowed a draft to blow on my girl, and so I closed it up tight.

Inch by inch, as though the house were a ship in dry dock, we overhauled the place, driven by concerns about Eva and then later, when our second child came

along, by concerns about Jesse. Who knew what cor-
rosion lurked in the heart of those old iron pipes? Re-
plumb with copper. Sparks from the fireplace might
leap through cracks in the chimney, so line it with
stainless steel and re-lay the bricks. Sand those oak
floors to protect small toes from splinters. And what if
there was lead in that peeling paint on the woodwork?
Better pry loose the baseboards and trim, the mold-
ings and sills, the mullioned windows; better carry it
all outdoors, then scrape and sand and strip everything
down to the bare wood, seal it anew with harmless fin-
ishes, and put every piece back where it belonged.

Like sap in maples, the urge to mend the house rises
in me with special force in spring. So it happens that I
am often hauling supplies up the front steps while
birds in our yard are gathering twigs and grass and
leaves. As I stagger to the door with a clutch of two-
by-fours on my shoulder, I see catbirds or cardinals or
robins laboring to their nests with loaded beaks.
Whenever I stop sawing or drilling, I am likely to hear
a chatter of construction from the trees. The link between their labor and mine is neither whimsical nor
quaint, but a matter of life and death. The river that
carries us along is wild, and we must caulk our boats to
keep afloat.

Unlike the birds, of course, we fetch our sticks from
the lumberyard, we get our mud ready-baked into
bricks, we buy fibers that have been woven into blan-
kets, curtains, carpets, mats. But for all that artifice,
the house is still entirely derived from the land. The
foundation is laid up with chunks of limestone from

nearby quarries. The frame is a skeleton of pines. The chairs once grew as hickory, their seats as cane and rush. The white walls are gypsum from the bed of a primeval sea. The iron in the nails has been refined from ore, the glass in the windows from sand, even the unavoidable plastic has been distilled from the oil of ancient swamps. When I walk up the stairs and notice the oak treads, I feel their grain curving through me.

Because so few of us build our own homes, we forget that our dwellings, like our bodies, are made from the earth. The first humans who settled in this part of the country fashioned their huts from bark, their tepees from tanned hides draped over poles. They warmed themselves at fires of buffalo chips and brush. How could they forget that they had wrapped themselves in the land? When white pioneers came to this region, a family would sometimes camp inside a hollow sycamore while they built a log cabin; so when at length they moved into the cabin, they merely exchanged life inside a single tree for life inside a stack of them. The bark on the walls and the clay in the chinks and the fieldstone in the chimney reminded them whence their shelter had come. Our technology has changed, but not our ultimate source. Even the newest ticky-tacky box in the suburbs, even the glitziest high tech mansion, even an aluminum trailer is only a nest in disguise.

Nature does not halt at the property line, but runs right through our yard and walls and bones. Possums and raccoons browse among kitchen scraps in the compost bin. Moss grows on the shady side of the roof, mildew in the bathtub, mold in the fridge. Roots from our front yard elm invade the drains. Mice invade the cupboards. (The best bait, we've found, is peanut butter.) Male woodpeckers, advertising for mates, rap on the cedar siding of the porch. Wrens nest in our kitchen exhaust fan, the racket of their hungry chicks spicing up our meals. Blue jays clack noisily in the gutters, turning over leaves in a search for bugs. Thousands of maples sprout from those gutters each spring. Water finds its way into the basement year round. For all our efforts to seal the joints, rain and snowmelt still treat the basement like any other hole in the ground.

When we bought the house, it was covered with English ivy. "That's got to come off," Ruth said. "Think of all the spiders breeding outside Eva's window!"

Under assault from crowbar, shears, and wire brush, the ivy came off. But there has been no perceptible decline in the spider population, indoors or out. Clean a corner, and by the time you've put away the broom, new threads are gleaming. The spiders thrive because they have plenty of game to snare. Poison has discouraged the termites, but carpenter ants still look upon the house as a convenient heap of dead wood. (When Eva first heard us talk about carpenter ants, she imagined they would be dressed as her daddy was on weekends, with sweatband across the forehead, tool belt around the waist, and dangling hammer on the hip.) Summer and fall, we play host to crickets, grasshoppers, moths, flies, mosquitoes, and frogs, along with no-see-ums too obscure to name.

Piled up foursquare and plumb, the house is not only composed from the land but is itself a part of the landscape. Weather buffets it, wind sifts through. Leaves collect on the roof, hemlock needles gather on the sills, ice and thaw nudge the foundation, seeds lodge in every crack. Like anything born, it is mortal. If you doubt that, drive the back roads of the Ohio Valley and look at the forsaken farms. Abandon a house, even a brick one such as ours, and it will soon be reclaimed by forest. Left to itself, the land says bloodroot, chickadee, beech. Our shelter is on loan; it needs perpetual care.

The word *house* derives from an Indo-European root meaning to cover or conceal. I hear in that etymology furtive, queasy undertones. Conceal from what? From storms? beasts? enemies? from the eye of God? *Home* comes from a different root meaning "the place where one lies." That sounds less fearful to me. A weak, slow, clawless animal, without fur or fangs, can risk lying down and closing its eyes only where it feels utterly secure. Since the universe is going to kill us, in the short run or the long, no wonder we crave a place to lie in safety, a place to conceive our young and raise them, a place to shut our eyes without shivering or dread.

Married seven years already at the time we bought our house, I forgot to carry Ruth over the threshold, but I did carry Eva, and when newborn Jesse came home from the hospital, I carried him as well. Whatever else crossing the threshold might symbolize— about property or patriarchy—it should mean that you have entered a place of refuge. Not a perfect refuge, for there is no such thing: disease can steal in, so can poison or thugs, hunger and pain. If the people who cross the threshold are bent or cruel, the rooms will fill with misery. No locks will keep armies out, no roof will hold against a tornado. No, not perfectly safe, yet home is where we go to hide from harm, or, having been hurt, to lick our wounds.

At 1113 East Wylie, we have no shrine in the yard, no hex sign on the gable, no horseshoe nailed over the door. But I sympathize with those who mark their houses with talismans to ward off evil. Our neighbors across the street have a small box mounted on their doorpost, a mezuza, which contains a slip of paper bearing words from Deuteronomy (6: 4–5): "Hear, O Israel: The Lord our God is one Lord; and you shall love the Lord your God with all your heart, and with all your soul, and with all your might." The words announce their faith, honor their God, and turn away the wicked. Each family, in its own manner, inscribes a visible or invisible message on its doorway, a message contrary to the one that Dante found over the gateway to Hell. Take hope, we say, rest easy, ye who enter here.

However leaky or firm, whether tar paper or brick, the shell of a house gives only shelter; a home gives sanctuary. Perhaps the most familiar definition of *home* in the American language comes from Robert Frost's "The Death of the Hired Man," in lines spoken by a Yankee farmer:

> "*Home is the place where, when you have to go there,*
> *They have to take you in.*"

Less familiar is the wife's reply:

> *"I should have called it*
> *Something you somehow haven't to deserve."*

The husband's remark is pure Yankee, grudging and grim. I side with the wife. Home is not where you *have* to go but where you *want* to go; nor is it a place where you are sullenly admitted, but rather where you are welcomed—by the people, the walls, the tiles on the floor, the flowers beside the door, the play of light, the very grass.

While I work on these pages, tucking in lines to make them tight, our newspaper carries an article with a grisly headline: HOMELESS WOMAN CRUSHED WITH TRASH. No one knows the woman's name, only that she crawled into a dumpster to sleep, was loaded into a truck, was compressed with the trash, and arrived dead at the incinerator. She wore white tennis shoes, gray sweatpants, red windbreaker, and, on her left hand, "a silver Indian Thunderbird ring." Nearby residents had seen her climb into the dumpster, and later they heard the truck begin to grind, but they did not warn the driver soon enough, and so the woman died. Being homeless meant that she had already been discarded by family, neighbors, and community, and now she was gathered with the trash. This happened in Indianapolis, just up the road from my snug house. I read the article twice; I read it a dozen times. I pinned the clipping to the wall beside my desk, and I keep returning to it as to a sore.

It *is* a sore, an affront, an outrage that thousands upon thousands of people in our country have nowhere to live. Like anyone who walks the streets of America, I grieve over the bodies wrapped in newspapers or huddled in cardboard boxes, the sleepers curled on steam grates, the futureless faces. This is cause for shame and remedy, not only because the homeless suffer, but because they have no place to lay their heads in safety, no one except dutiful strangers to welcome them. Thank God for dutiful strangers; yet they can never take the place of friends. The more deeply I feel my own connection to home, the more acutely I feel the hurt of those who belong to no place and no one.

The longing for a safe place to lie down echoes through our holy songs and scriptures. Abused and scorned, we look over Jordan, and what do we see? A band of angels coming for to carry us home. If earth has no room for us, we are promised, then heaven will. The string of assurances in the Twenty-third Psalm ends with the most comforting one of all:

> *Surely goodness and mercy shall follow me*
> *all the days of my life;*
> *and I shall dwell in the house of the Lord*
> *for ever.*

If we are ever going to dwell in the house of the Lord, I believe, we do so now. If any house is divinely made, it is this one here, this great whirling mansion of planets and stars.

Each constellation of the zodiac is said to live in its own house, Leo and Libra and Aquarius, and so on through all the twelve that ride the merry-go-round of our year. I do not believe that our future is written in the sky. And yet there is some truth in sketching houses around the stars. Viewed from chancy earth, they appear to be stay-at-homes, abiding in place from generation to generation, secure beyond our imagining. And if the constellations belong in their houses so beautifully and faithfully, then so might we.

In baseball, home plate is where you begin your journey and also your destination. You venture out onto the bases, to first and second and third, always striving to return to the spot from which you began. There is danger on the basepath—pick-offs, rundowns, force-outs, double plays—and safety only back at home. I am not saying, as a true fan would, that baseball is the key to life; rather, life is the key to baseball. We play or watch this game because it draws pictures of our desires.

The homing pigeon is not merely able to find the roost from astounding distances; the pigeon *seeks* its home. I am a homing man. Away on solo trips, I am never quite whole. I miss family, of course, and neighbors and friends; but I also miss the house, which is planted in the yard, which is embraced by a city, which is cradled in familiar woods and fields, which gather snow and rain for the Ohio River. The house has worked on me as steadily as I have worked on the house. I carry slivers of wood under my fingernails, dust from demolition in the corners of my eyes, aches from hammering and heaving in all my joints.

During my lifetime the labels *homemaker* and *housewife* have come to seem belittling, as though a woman who wears them lacks the gumption to be anything else. A similar devaluation hit the word *homely* itself, which originally meant plain, simple, durable, worthy of use in the home, and gradually came to mean drab, graceless, ugly. Men can now be called househusbands, but the male variant, like the female, is used apologetically, as though qualified by the word *only*.

In a recent letter, a friend wrote me, "I'm still just a househusband; but I'm looking for work." I'd be surprised if there wasn't plenty of work to do in his own house. It's a rare home that couldn't do with more care. Wendell Berry warns us about that need in his poem "The Design of a House":

> *Except in idea, perfection is as wild*
> *as light; there is no hand laid on it.*
> *But the house is a shambles*
> *unless the vision of its perfection*
> *upholds it like stone.*

Our rooms will only be as generous and nurturing as the spirit we invest in them. The Bible gives us the same warning, more sternly: Unless God builds the house, it will not stand. The one I live in has been standing for just over sixty years, a mere eyeblink, not long enough to prove there was divinity in the mortar. I do know, however, that mortar and nails alone would not have held the house together even for sixty years. It has also needed the work of many hands, the wishes of many hearts, vision upon vision, through a succession of families.

Real estate ads offer houses for sale, not homes. A house is a garment, easily put off or on, casually bought and sold; a home is skin. Merely change houses and you will be disoriented; change homes and you bleed. When the shell you live in has taken on the savor of your love, when your dwelling has become a taproot, then your house is a home.

I heard more than hunger in Eva's infant cry. I heard a plea for shelter from the terror of things. I felt called on to enfold her, in arms and walls and voice. No doubt it is only a musical accident that *home* and *womb* share the holy sound of *om*, which Hindu mystics chant to put themselves in harmony with the ultimate power. But I accept all gifts of language. There is in the word a hum of yearning.

Since Eva went off to college, I find it hard not to think of our home as a chrysalis from which the butterfly has flown. I miss my daughter. The rug bristles with the absence of her dancing feet. The windows glint with the history of her looking. Water rings on the sills recall where her teacup should be. The air lacks a sweet buzz.

Unlike a butterfly, a daughter blessedly returns now and again, as Eva comes home soon for summer vacation. Ruth and I have been preparing the house to receive her. Before leaving in August, Eva bet me that I would not have finished remodeling the sun porch by the time of her return in May. I stole hours to work on it all the autumn and winter. Now I must go and put on the last coat of varnish, so that, when she enters, the room will shine.

CHAPTER THREE

EARTH'S BODY

SEAL TIGHT YOUR ROOF
and walls and they will shelter you from weather, but they will not shield you from fear. Fear comes on me now in this twitching hour between midnight and dawn. I cannot say exactly which hour, because I am afraid to look at a clock. My back aches and shoulders throb from splitting a cord of oak, which was a foolish way for a man of forty-six to spend a day in August. Here in southern Indiana, August is a slow oven. The bones bake, the blood thins, the mind oozes into holes.

Even with windows gaping, the house catches no breeze. The only stir of breath comes from my wife, my daughter, my son, and me. Kept awake by the heat or my panicky heart, I tossed for a spell on damp sheets, cooking in my own juice, until dread snatched me out of bed. I put on a loose pair of shorts, all the clothing I could bear, and crept downstairs. Now I huddle in the kitchen, the lights on, tea steeping. I trace the grain in the table—also oak, like the wood I split all day—running my finger along the curved lines as though one of them might lead me out of the pit.

Surely you know the place I am talking about. You have skidded down the slope toward oblivion, for shorter or longer stays. And so you realize the pit is not a gap in something solid, like a hole in rock, but the absence of all solidity, the square root of nowhere and nothing. I go there too often, never willingly, usually dragged from bed by the scruff of my neck.

A dog will bite a rag and shake it, first playfully, then earnestly, and at last furiously, with snarls and bristling hair, as though outraged by the limp cloth. Just so, in the dark hours, certainty of death seizes me by the throat. The grip is hesitant to begin with, a teasing nibble, then the teeth clamp tight and I am lifted and shaken like the flimsiest rag. It is a dance I have known since childhood, this midnight shimmy with dread, and yet each time it sweeps me up my belly churns and muscles jerk as though for the first time. Nothing else in my life—not the tang of blackberries or the perfume of lilacs, not even the smack of love—is so utterly fresh, so utterly convincing, as this fear of annihilation.

Such alarm over the quenching of mind's wavery flame! Is this any way for a grown man to feel? Suitable or not, it is what I do feel. I rehearse this midnight panic because I cannot separate the bright thread of fear from the story I have to tell, which is about making oneself at home on the earth, knowing the earth as one body knows another.

I sip the tea while staring at the kitchen window. The glass gives back the reflection of a balding man with taut lips, shadows in the hollows of cheeks and in gashes beside a crooked nose, black sockets where the eyes should be. No comfort there. The image is thinner and more fragile than the glass on which it hovers. I shift in my chair and the face disappears.

I raise a hand to my cheek, feel the stubble of whiskers, the slick of sweat, the nub of skull. Stubborn, those whiskers. Shaved morning after morning, they are not discouraged. They will persevere after my heart and lungs have quit. I take a dish towel from the drawer, sniff sunlight in the air-dried cloth, and wipe my face. Immediately the sweat begins to bead again, on skin that draws closer each year to the contours of the skull.

If you are older than thirty or so, you have shared this moment. You have studied the cracks in your face, the slump in your belly, the leaching of color from your hair. You have traced erosion under the tips of your fingers and in the icy pools of mirrors. No perception is more commonplace; and no emotion is more futile than fussing about it. Like any tree or hill, like any house heaved up into the weather, our bodies wear down. Inside the furrowing skin, slowly but implacably, nerves unravel, cell walls buckle, messages go astray. Like gravity, like entropy, the rules of decay are printed in small type on our ticket of admission into the world.

The body is scarcely more durable than the reflection of a shadowy face in the night window. So where am I to turn during these unclocked hours before dawn? If there is no room for hope in the cramped house of the skin, and no security in the glimmerings of the mind, then what abides? Does anything persist, any knot more stubborn than bone, any force more steadfast than thought? The question drives me to set down my mug of tea, extinguish the kitchen light, and go outside into the dark.

I might have walked into a cave, the dark is so deep. No light shines from the neighboring houses, nor from the moon, long since gone down, nor from the stars, blanked out by clouds. My eyes could be shut, for all the news they gather. Descending the steps into our back yard, I push against the darkness as against the weight of black water.

My eyes may be empty, but my ears quickly fill. The air sizzles with insect song. Crickets and grasshoppers warn and woo, rubbing their musical legs. They make the sound of beans rattling in a pan, tiny bells ringing on the ankles of dancers, fingers raked over the teeth of combs, waves rolling cobbles on the shore. Dozens of species combine to make this amorous hullabaloo. If I were to focus on the chirp of the snowy tree cricket, as one might pick out the oboe from an orchestra, and if I were to count the number of beats in fifteen seconds, then add that number to thirty-seven, the sum would roughly equal the temperature in Fahrenheit. I have tried this many times, and insect and thermometer usually agree within a few degrees. But on this muggy night I do not care to know the temperature, much as I admire the crickets for keeping track.

I hear no human sounds, amorous or otherwise, except the brief wail of a baby and the long wail of a siren. Cats bicker, without much enthusiasm. Now and again birds pipe up fretfully, as if reminding all within earshot that their trees are occupied. They will not be singing for some while yet. When baby, siren, cats, and birds fall silent, the insects own the air.

Listening, I cease to feel the weight of black water. I let myself walk out onto the lawn, trusting that the earth will uphold me, even though I cannot see the ground. The soil, baked hard by August, is lumpy under my bare feet. It smells of dust, dry and dull, as though it has never known the lushness of spring. The brittle grass licks my soles with a thousand feathery tongues. From the depths of my churchly childhood, the words of Isaiah (40: 6–8) rise up:

> *All flesh is grass,*
>   *and all its beauty is like the flower of the field.*
> *The grass withers, the flower fades,*
>   *when the breath of the Lord blows upon it;*
>   *surely the people is grass.*
> *The grass withers, the flower fades;*
>   *but the word of our God will stand for ever.*

Whoever composed that verse must have spent time down in the pit, wondering what does not fade, what will stand forever.

In lines that are familiar even to the unchurchly, Jesus converted Isaiah's warning into a promise: "Consider the lilies, how they grow; they neither toil nor spin; yet I tell you, even Solomon in all his glory was not arrayed like one of these. But if God so clothes the grass which is alive in the field today and tomorrow is thrown into the oven, how much more will he clothe you, O men of little faith!" (Luke 12:27–28). Indeed, grass has been well clothed for more than a hundred million years. Persistent, nourishing grass! Brother to corn, sister to rice, cousin to wheat! In the darkness, the voices of Isaiah and Jesus speak to me like rival angels, one saying *Look how grass withers under the breath of August*, the other saying *Yes, but look how it pushes up numberless fresh blades each May*.

My frisky mind keeps darting off, loping through a lifetime of books, raiding memory, jumping ahead into the future, visiting countries where I have never set foot, zigzagging through the cosmos. And why not? When the fiddling of a cricket is tuned to the temperature, which is driven by the weather, which is linked to the earth's tilting spin, which is governed by all the matter in the universe, why shouldn't one's mind gambol about? Only risky, roving thought can be adequate to such a world.

While my mind rushes hither and yon, however, my body stays put. For the flesh there is no past or future, there is only this instant of contact, here, now. Heart pumps. Muscles twitch. Ears fill with indecipherable song. I lift my face and swallow some of the boggy air. With it comes the fruity smell of oak, released like a long held secret from the pile of split logs. I smell the rank sweetness of the compost bin, where apple cores and watermelon rinds deliquesce back toward dirt. I stroke the limestone blocks that hem in the wildflower bed. The flowers have faded but the stones endure, sandpapery to the touch. All the while, August heat clings to my limbs like damp wool.

As my eyes open their shutters to the dark, I dimly make out the twin trunks of our backyard maples. I shuffle to the nearer tree and read the braille of the bark with my fingers. Roots hump beneath my feet. Overhead, leaves form a canopy of black lace. I press my cheek and chest against the sharp ridges of the bark and wrap my arms around the trunk. My hands do not meet, the maple is so stout.

Once again, my mind sets off on its rambles. I remember hugging my Mississippi grandmother, her dresses made from flour sacking, her waist larger than the circle of my child's arms. I think of the goitrous, trembling, marvelous woman who taught me in high school biology class the parts of trees—heartwood and sapwood, phloem and cambium, stomata, rootlet, bud. I remember stroking the creamy flanks of sycamores on the banks of the Mahoning before that river was dammed. I think of the women in northern India who preserved their forest from loggers by hugging trees. Over our dead bodies, the women said, and meant it. Their struggle came to be known as *Chipko*, a Hindi expression meaning "embrace our trees."

If Ruth were to wake and come to the window and see me clasping a maple, would she be jealous? Would she fear losing me to the wood nymphs? Would she think I had become a druid? Or would she merely laugh at her ridiculous, moody husband? I do the laughing for her. My guffaw spreads ripples of silence through the crowd of insects. The spell broken, I unclasp the tree and stand back, hitching up my baggy shorts. I am comforted, although by whom or what I cannot say.

Comforted, I lie down on the lawn, and the blades prick the skin of my back and legs. I loaf and invite my soul. It is too dark for observing a spear of summer grass, yet I cannot help but remember Whitman's *Song of Myself*:

> *A child said* What is the grass? *fetching it to me with full hands;*
> *How could I answer the child? I do not know what it is any more than he.*

Grass might be "the beautiful uncut hair of graves," Whitman speculates, yet he goes on to affirm that

> *The smallest sprout shows there is really no death,*
> *And if ever there was it led forward life, and does not wait at the end to arrest it,*
> *And ceas'd the moment life appear'd.*
> *All goes onward and outward, nothing collapses,*
> *And to die is different from what any one supposed, and luckier.*

Instead of whistling in the dark, I sing. Lying there on my six feet of earth, I am reassured not so much by Whitman's words as by the shapely energy they appeal to—the chorusing crickets, the surging trees, the vigorous grass. My skin carries the bite marks of bark. My throat carries the aroma of cooking compost. My ears ring with the night gossip of birds. The darkness brims over with life. Thus I scratch my way up out of the pit into the arms of the world.

As I enter the kitchen, the clock—no longer terrifying—chimes four. I have been in the yard long enough for my tea to cool to the sultry temperature of the air. I carry the mug back outside and sit at the picnic table to wait for dawn to pump light into the world.

There is a species of poem called an *aubade*, which is a morning song, usually a lament of lovers forced to part at dawn, although it may be merely a celebration of sunrise, as in these lines from Robert Browning:

> *The year's at the spring,*
> *And day's at the morn;*
> *Morning's at seven;*
> *The hill-side's dew-pearled;*
> *The lark's on the wing;*
> *The snail's on the thorn;*
> *God's in His heaven—*
> *All's right with the world!*

I know that little lyric because it was stitched in red on a sampler that hung upon the wall of my childhood bedroom. I read those lines a thousand times as I lay in bed, terrified of sleep, wondering if I would ever wake, wondering if the world would still be there at dawn, trying to persuade myself that I would surface again from the black water and that morning would clean up whatever mess had been left by the previous day.

We didn't have larks where I grew up, but we did have roosters to announce the day, as well as dew to glisten and thorns to bristle and snails to leave opalescent tracks in the first light. So my midwestern mornings were charged with as much hope and grandeur as any English morning witnessed by Robert Browning. But my neighborhood had more troubling features as well—including bombs and bullies, suicides and drunks—that led me to doubt whether all really was right with the world. Amid the tumult of my teenage years, when I became certain that much in the world was miserably wrong, the lyric lost its charm, and God moved from heaven without leaving a forwarding address. Ever since, I have been trying to find where divinity resides.

Which brings me to the other sort of dawn song, the erotic verses that do not appear in red stitches on children's bedroom walls. *Aubade* is a French word pronounced roughly "oh-bod," and that is also roughly what it means. Oh bod! Glorious, desirable body! Not all examples are suitable for family entertainment, but there is a mild and famous one in *Romeo and Juliet.* The young lovers, secretly married, have spent their first night together—offstage—and as the scene opens Juliet is pleading:

> *Wilt thou be gone? it is not yet near day:*
> *It was the nightingale, and not the lark,*
> *That pierced the fearful hollow of thine ear;*
> *Nightly she sings on yond pomegranate-tree:*
> *Believe me, love, it was the nightingale.*

Whether it is actually dawn or not is of some consequence to Romeo because he has been exiled for killing
a man and must depart the realm before daylight on
pain of death. Thus he replies:

> *It was the lark, the herald of the morn,*
> *No nightingale: look, love, what envious streaks*
> *Do lace the severing clouds in yonder east:*
> *Night's candles are burnt out, and jocund day*
> *Stands tiptoe on the misty mountain tops.*
> *I must be gone and live, or stay and die.*

Juliet insists that dawn is not breaking, and Romeo
says, very well, I'll stay, death is a small price to pay for
a few more minutes of bliss; whereupon she admits
that it really is day and bids him go. He does go, after
another exchange of metaphors, and the lovers are re-
united only once again, and even more famously, in
the tomb.

Dawn delivers me from the tomb. Nightly I am under sentence of death, and daily the sentence is relaxed.
Not revoked, mind you—merely stayed. In the darkness, I cling to trees, dig my fingers in the dirt, to keep
from being dragged away. In the brightness I can ease
my grip. Sun resurrects the weighty world. A king reveals his royalty, a saint her holiness, by restoring
sight to the blind. Just so, the dawn for me is holy
balm.

This dawn, the one I wait for at the picnic table,
comes stealthily. Clouds diffuse the sunrise. No
bucket of yellow spills over the eastern horizon, but

instead light seeps evenly through the whole dome, as if the sky were on a rheostat. Against the gathering brightness, the fretted edges of trees, the tangle of poles and wires, and the roof lines of my neighbors' houses begin to show. It is not so wild a landscape as the one I touched in the darkness, yet neither is it wholly tame. The crickets keep wooing. Crows and jays banter raucously as they flounce from perch to perch. Bats, not yet ready to call it a night, flicker by on the trail of mosquitoes. Black-eyed Susans stare, tomatoes ripen, rhubarb wags its elephant ears. Beside the rhubarb patch a blue spruce, planted there after bearing our tinsel indoors one Christmas, extrudes fresh needles from the tips of twigs. A squirrel slinks onto a limb over my head to fuss at me for invading the yard. All of this—not to mention the work of worms under my feet, the bacteria in my belly, the rising of the sun itself—goes on without anybody's say-so. Power lines and roof lines banish the eagles, alas, along with the fringed gentian, the grizzly, and the faint tracery of comets, but they do not shut out, cannot shut out, the greater life by which we live. Dawn gives back to my eyes this delectable presence. If Ruth has reason to be jealous, it is not of another woman, nor of a dryad, but of the seductive creation.

Earth is sexy, just as sex is earthy. Each of us is a landscape of plains and peaks, valleys and thickets. I speak in metaphors, as through a garbled phone line, but what I mean is plain and simple: body and land are one flesh. They are made of the same stuff. Their beauty is one beauty, their wounds the same wounds. They call to us in the same perennial voice, crying,

Come see, come touch, come listen and smell, and O come taste. We explore them alike, honor or abuse them alike. The health or sickness of one is inseparable from that of the other. There is no division between where we live and what we are.

The boys I knew while growing up in farm country spoke appreciatively about the lay of the land and spoke boastfully about this girl or that as a good lay, thereby confusing two passions. Such confusion—along with the whole sad history of men bullying women and animals and soil—has led some earnest people to conclude that the earth *is* female, innocent and fruitful, and not only in the imaginations of adolescent boys. To claim the earth as female might well make women feel powerful, a worthy consequence, but it also has the effect of making men seem like intruders on the planet. The claim is false, as well as dangerous. My body, no less than my wife's, is made of the earth. The radioactivity in my bones still ticks from the formation of the planet. Like Ruth, I carry within me the legacy of a thousand generations of genes. In my moody cycles, along with all other men, I might even be swayed by the moon—the scientists are still debating that point. I am certainly swayed by sunrise and starfire, by wind and rain, by my fellow creatures, by the whole procession of the year. I belong here, and so do we all, men and women.

Earth is our mother, as even bumper stickers remind us, but it is also our father; it is our brother and sister, husband and wife, male as well as female. In loving this gorgeous planet, we are freed from the half-life, the polarity of gender. I do not mean to belittle the marriage of man and woman, which is a joy to me, but to enlarge it. We think of sex too narrowly, as though it were a mere magnetism of groin to groin. The sensuous attraction that pulls us into bed is a special case of the greater attraction that binds us, nerves and belly and brain, to the flesh of the earth.

I realize it may seem odd to others that I find the earth voluptuous. But there it is. What am I to make of it? I have never been tempted to go naked to a party or to bask in the buff on a crowded beach. When a Supreme Court justice remarked not long ago that a society of nudists might wish to rent the Hoosierdome in Indianapolis and convene there in the altogether—acres of skin in plastic seats—I did not find the prospect enticing. But I have often felt like shucking my clothes on the peaks of mountains, in the privacy of rivers, in the shadowy depths of woods. Not only felt like it, I am bound to confess, but have done so, when weather and solitude permitted. Psychiatrists may well have a label for this impulse, since they have a label for most of our desires, healthy or otherwise. Without benefit of a label, I acknowledge the impulse as part of who I am.

I first disrobed in the wild at the age of five, soon after my family had moved into the arsenal, that paradise of bombs, where deer were as common as rabbits. One afternoon I came upon a fawn bedded down in the woods behind our house. The deer, no bigger than I was, did not know enough to fear me, and so it lay there observing me calmly with slick brown eyes. It wore only a birthday suit of dappled fur, which invited my fingers, and I felt a powerful urge to cuddle against that tawny creature in my own birthday suit of simple skin. And so, there being at the age of five fewer barricades between wish and act, I wriggled out of my clothes and knelt down and lay my head on the velvety fur. The fawn shivered but did not bolt. I was launched on a lifetime of courtship.

I have not met another fawn on such intimate terms. Now and again, however, and well beyond the age of five—right up to my present age, in fact—I have been lured out of my clothes by waterfalls or wildflowers or stars. By giving in to this urge I have broken the laws of several states, ranging from Maine to Oregon. Before undressing, I always make sure there are no sheriffs in the vicinity—nor anybody else, for that matter, since I do not wish to impose my rapture on strangers. It *is* rapture. When I first read *King Lear* and I came to the storm scene on the heath where the crazed old man, already stripped of the crown by his own hand, shouts "Off, off, you lendings!" and begins tearing at his clothes, I understood his frenzy. He has lost his kingdom, lost his daughters, all but lost his mind. What pleasures, what consolations remain for him except those that flow in through the channels of the senses? In grief or joy, a hard rain and a wild field call for peeling away the husks, stripping down to what Lear calls the "poor, bare, forked animal" of the body. My house is surrounded by scruffy lawns and buckled sidewalks, nothing so desolate as a heath. Near home I keep my clothes on, out of regard for my neighbors, and yet no thunderstorm passes without tempting me to dance naked in the street.

No promise of thunderstorms today, alas. Dry, dry, and hot. Between the withered blades of grass in my yard the dirt has cracked. Even in the heat, numberless lives still burn in the air and wood and soil, and I still feel a yen to get up and dance. So I do. My shorts are floppy as a clown's, my shuffle as clumsy. I am no Lear, no Romeo, neither hero nor king, merely a man who aches from a day of splitting wood and a night of fear and longing. The lover I dance with seems not to care.

In the memorable phrasing of The Letter to the Hebrews (11: 1), "faith is the assurance of things hoped for, the conviction of things not seen." By that measure, and by most others, I am a man of little faith. In the dark night of the soul, I reach out to assure myself of things not seen. I must lay my hands on the side of the tree, must feel the prick of grass on my skin, must smell the dirt, must sing to myself a brave lullaby in order to sustain my hopes.

What do I hope for? Eternal life, I suppose. By that I mean something besides immortality—although, like all creatures not maddened by pain, I am hooked on the habit of living. The eternal life I seek is not some after time, some other place, but awareness of eternity in this moment and this place. What I crave is contact with the force that moves and shapes all there is or has been or will be.

The earth and our own bodies, by casting shadows, seem to be the opposite of light. But if you have gazed up through the leaves of a tree at the sky, if you have watched the jeweled crests of waves, or held a shimmering fish in your hand, or lifted your palm against the sun and seen ruby light blazing through the flesh of your squeezed fingers, you know that matter is filled with fire. Matter *is* fire, in slow motion. Einstein taught us as much, and bomb testers keep proving it with cataclysmic explosions. The resistant stuff we touch and walk on and eat, the resistant stuff we are, blood and bone, is not the opposite of light but light's incarnation.

The Taoist book of wisdom, *The Secret of the Golden Flower*, speaks about a condition of utter clarity and selflessness as "living midnight." I don't know a word of the original Chinese, and I might well misread the translation, but I am haunted by this phrase. Living midnight: to face oblivion, to drown in the annihilating water, to dwell without fear or fret at the still center. Hardest of all is to live *through* midnight, to accept the knowledge of one's own private extinction and still return to daylight charged with passion and purpose.

The man who dances in the backyard with an invisible lover, and then comes in the house humming to breakfast with his family, is the same one who was shaken like a rag by dread in the depths of the night.

"Hi, Pop," Eva says as I enter the kitchen.

"Morning, old guy," says Jesse.

"Did you have a bad night?" asks Ruth, who notices whenever I leave bed early.

"Not so bad," I answer, and then, considering, I add, "a good night, really."

I kiss their shining heads, each in turn. Their faces, so dear and mysterious, tilt up at me. Their skin glows from sleep. No, not only from sleep. They glow steadily, my wife and daughter and son, this morning as always, with a radiance that my wakefulness helps me to see.

This is no happy ending, merely an interlude, a reprieve. My vision will dim once more, and I will have to clear my sight. Dread will seize me by the throat. When the need comes on me, I will go outside.

The sudden fierce grip of fear was once thought to be the mischievous work of Pan, the god of wildness, and thus we still speak of feeling panic. I may be perverse, but I find myself soothed rather than frightened by wildness. I am reassured to feel one juice flowing through my fingers and the branches of the maple and the flickering grass. Pantheism has taken a beating since the rise of the great monotheistic religions. I believe there is only one power, one shaping urge, but I also believe that it infuses everything—the glistening track of the snail along with the gleaming eye of the fawn, the grain in the oak, the froth on the creek, the coiled proteins in my blood and in yours, the mind that strings together these words and the mind that reads them.

The only sure antidote to oblivion is the creation. So I loop my sentences around the trunks of maples, hook them into the parched soil, anchor them to rock, to moon and stars, wrap them tenderly around the ankles of those I love. From down in the pit I give a tug, to make sure my rope of words is firmly hooked into the world, and then up I climb.

CHAPTER FOUR

THE
FORCE
OF
MOVING
WATER

As I watched Eva being born, and this new creature emerged, wet and glistening, into the difficult air, it seemed to me that baby and mother and I were riding a powerful river. The three of us had been caught and lifted and hurled by wave upon wave, driven on by an irresistible current. After the delivery, Eva sleeping and Ruth beaming, we drifted into a stretch of quiet water. Yet even then I felt the tug of the river, and I have continued to feel it during the years since Eva's birth, the current sometimes gentle and sometimes fierce, but always there, bearing us along.

Watching Eva enter the world, and then, a few years later, watching newborn Jesse, I understood more deeply than ever before my love for water. We all ride the river, we are all born from a sack of water, and some of us never quit hankering for that original wet-ness. From birth onward, we are drawn to the wash of lakes, the heave of oceans, the hustle of streams, the needling drum of rain. I hike miles to see a creek slide over ledges, I gaze like a soothsayer into ponds, I slip into a daze from the sound of drizzle on the roof. When it storms and the street is running like a sluice, I go out barefoot or booted and slosh about while neighbors stare at me from the shelter of porches.

When Eva and Jesse were little, they would often dash into the cloudbursts with me, and we would take long shivery walks through the downpour. We built dams in the gutter, laid our ears against storm grates to hear the underground roar, raced sticks on the swollen brook in the park. I would come back inside the house tingling. There are souls—including many saints—who feel at home in deserts, but I am not one of them. I am strictly a wetlands man. I crave the company of water, any water, above all the meander and surge of rivers.

The river I have come to know most familiarly, the river that winds through the center of my imagination as it winds through my region, is the Ohio. I was born next to a larger one, the great brown flood into which the Ohio pours, the Old Man himself, the Mississippi. I remember dragging a gunny sack behind me down the rows of cotton in a field near Memphis when I was a toddler not much taller than the bushes, remember coming to the steep bank of a levee, climbing to the top and then finding spread before me the mile-wide muddy water. It might have been an ocean, for all I could see of the far shore. The very earth seemed to have turned liquid. I knew what it was, of course, because the slick brown river was my most famous neighbor, the Father of Waters. I knew stories about the way it sometimes stirred in its bed and cut a new channel or snatched houses and trees and unwary toddlers in its wet claws. I could even spell its long snaky name, chanting the jingle, "Em-I-ess-ess-I-ess-ess-I-pee-pee-I." Looking out over that rolling flood from the levee, I was mesmerized and terrified. Rivers still affect me that way. Anybody who is not a bit scared by a river has either not looked at a real one or not looked hard enough.

About the time I learned to shape the letters of Mississippi with a fat pencil, my family moved north into the vicinity of a new river. I dozed in Kentucky and woke to the rumble of our car tires on the bridge leading from Covington into Cincinnati. A bridge meant water, so I stuck my head out the window and peered down between steel girders. What I saw looked smaller than the Mississippi, tamer, less muddy, but for all that it was still impressive. My mother told me its name, only four letters, easy to spell: O-hi-o. Except for time spent elsewhere studying and traveling, I have lived ever since in the watershed of this river. After all these years of riding beside or upon it, learning about it, carrying its great muscular body in my mind, there is a part of me that runs night and day with the Ohio.

Chances are, your own life and the history of your place are braided with the current of a river, as my life and place are braided with the Ohio. When we figure our addresses, we might do better to forget zip codes and consider where the rain goes after it falls outside our windows. We need such knowledge, need to feel as intimate with the branching and gathering of the earth's veins as we do with the veins in our own wrists. The tilt of land that snares the rain also defines where we *are* more profoundly than any state line or city limit. States often draw their borders along rivers, yet that is false to the land because rivers join rather than divide their two shores. My rumpled neighborhood in southern Indiana has more to do with the hill country across the river in Kentucky than it does with the glacial plains of northern Indiana. Nature ignores our political boundaries. Birds migrate up and down the valleys, seeds ride the currents, plants colonize outward from the banks, and all manner of beasts—including humans—seek homes and food and one another along the paths of rivers. A true map of our continent would show a pattern of curving watersheds stitched together along high ridges, like a paisley fabric.

The watershed of the Ohio stretches into fourteen states, including ones as far afield as New York, Maryland, and Alabama, draining an area that is roughly the size of France. The basin reaches from the Appalachian Mountains in the east to the Illinois prairies in the west, from the Great Lakes in the north to the Great Smoky Mountains in the south. Two sizable rivers, the Monongahela and Allegheny, give rise to the Ohio at Pittsburgh, and before it empties into the Mississippi at Cairo, almost a thousand miles later, it gathers in dozens of tributaries, including the Muskingum, Kanawha, Scioto, Big Sandy, Great and Little Miami, Kentucky, Green, Wabash, Cumberland, and Tennessee. Its width varies from seven hundred feet in the upper reaches to nearly a mile at the mouth. In low stages, it pours twenty-two thousand cubic feet of water into the Mississippi every second, and in flood it pours sixteen hundred thousand per second, an amount that would cover a football field to the height of a four-story building. Those flood waters can be as muddy as the Old Man's, but generally the Ohio is clearer, slow to mix with the "thick and yaller" current of the Mississippi, as Mark Twain observed. Depending on the light, the season, and the stage of the river, the water can remind you of coffee with cream, the amber of tobacco juice, the green of moss, the lavender of lilacs, or robin's egg blue; or the surface can become a liquid mirror, doubling the islands and hills.

Swimming in the Ohio, I try to feel all the remotest creeks of that vast basin trickling through me. I like to imagine I can smell in the river the pines from the mountains, the oaks and hickories of the foothills, the blackberries and wildflowers of the bottomlands. What I'm likelier to smell is diesel oil, cotton poison, coal slurry, or sewage, because twenty-five million people live in the basin, and the watercourses are lined with towns, factories, mills, slag heaps, power plants, and refineries. Like the rest of our planet, the Ohio is caught in a tug-of-war between natural influences and human ones.

From bluffs along the river, you gaze down on a quintessential American landscape: a low island in mid-channel, half woods and half overgrown pasture surrounding the tumbled foundations of barns; coal-filled barges churning past, some headed for power plants whose cooling towers and smokestacks bristle around the next bend; other barges heaped with corn or steel or automobiles, lashed to docks for unloading by conveyors and long-armed derricks; beyond the docks, a scramble of railroad tracks, high tension wires, gas lines, roads, our own channels of power following the river's; in the bottomlands, clapboard farm houses, some in ruins and some in restored glory; dented trailers with dish antennas and woodpiles and cannibalized cars in the yards; inlets marked by the white blaze of sycamores; fields of tobacco and soybeans; a chemical plant spewing gray smoke; hills illumined by redbud and the blue pokers of larkspur; mud lots gouged by hogs, meadows grazed by cows; old cellar holes outlined by the persistent blooms of jonquils and forsythia; glacial sand and gravel pits; the spires and boxy shoulders of white frame churches; and on the ridge against the sky a whiskery fringe of trees. It is a landscape at once pastoral and industrial, wild and tame. The river is a sovereign power only half bound in the chains of our purposes. We exist as a people in that tension, loving wildness and fearing it, longing for contact with untrammeled nature and at the same time longing for control.

The Ohio has concentrated our desires and designs as it has concentrated the waters of a hundred streams. Because it was the principal avenue of settlement leading west from the colonies on the Atlantic seaboard, the history of our dealings with the Ohio epitomize our dealings with the continent as a whole. By dumping our wastes into the water, building dams and locks and bridges, raising levees, charting every point and riffle and bar, we have superimposed ourselves onto the river. Only by consulting old records and resorting to imagination can we glimpse what the Ohio might have been like apart from our tinkering.

Humans have lived beside the Ohio for virtually all of its history. It is young as rivers go, only some ten or fifteen thousand years. When the last glaciers crunched down over the Midwest, they blocked the north-flowing streams. These trapped streams and the glacier's own meltwater scoured westward, cutting through ridges of limestone and sandstone and coal-rich shale, gouging fresh channels and joining together pieces of ancient riverbeds, eventually producing the modern Ohio, which is a sort of twisted rag rope of old and new. And I do mean twisted: while the river drifts generally southwest, there are stretches where within a few miles it flows toward every point of the compass. If it were a crow instead of a stream, the Ohio would cover the distance between Pittsburgh and Cairo in only half as many miles. The other half it spends meandering.

In cutting through bedrock, the turbulent new river exposed to view the fossils of sea creatures—dazzling corkscrews, hinged shells like the wings of angels, armored trilobites, entire coral reefs. Rambling along the Ohio in 1810, Zadok Cramer—author of *The Navigator*, the standard early guide to the river—noticed "the very singular manner in which the rocks were filled with appearances of animal and vegetable substances, marine shells, particularly the cockle; the whole shape of a bird, in form like the bat; the butter-fly, &c." Well before geologists explained these mysterious shapes, Cramer was shrewd enough

> to suppose this country was once a great sea or lake, either of fresh or salt water, and that these sub-stances, after the great convulsion of nature which occasioned dry land to appear, were thrown together in the struggle, and being exposed to a different element, from animated and soft vegetable bodies, Time, the moulder of Nature's matter, has shaped them into massy rocks, as we now find them.

Indeed, a shallow ocean occupied the heart of the continent for tens of millions of years, and the newly spawned Ohio carved a channel through the ancient sediments.

After the ice vanished, the river remained, and soon plants flung their net of green over the boggy shores, arborvitaes and sedges, spruces and firs. Pockets of those cold-loving species can still be found in the valley on north-facing slopes and in frosty hollows. The plants were followed by animals, including such lumbering brutes as musk oxen, giant beavers, saber-toothed tigers, and woolly mammoths. The remains of these creatures have shown up at Big Bone Lick, just south of the river below Cincinnati. Visiting that muddy site early in the nineteenth century, the ornithologist Alexander Wilson "found numerous fragments of large bones lying scattered about. In pursuing a wounded duck across this quagmire, I had nearly deposited my carcass among the grand congregation of mammoths below, having sunk up to the middle, and had hard struggling to get out."

Less respectful travelers used the gigantic ribs and tusks for tent poles or gate posts. Ever-curious about the western lands, President Jefferson sent William Clark to perform a dig at Big Bone Lick in 1807— likely the first paleontological expedition in our hemisphere—and Clark, who had returned only the previous year from his epic journey to the Pacific with Meriwether Lewis, duly shipped three hundred bones to the White House. Some of the specimens made their way into collections in Europe, where they provoked naturalists to speculate anew about the history of life. More recent digs at Big Bone Lick have turned up the fossils of mastodons, peccaries, ground sloths, tapirs, and gigantic elk.

The four-legged beasts were succeeded by two-legged ones, the hunters, fishers, and planters. Through overzealous hunting, in fact, these human newcomers may have contributed to the extinction of the great mammals. The earliest settlers along the Ohio were descendants of those who crossed over from Asia, the original American immigrants hungry for land. I like to think of them in their skins and shrewdness coming upon the raw swollen river while the retreating wall of ice was still visible on the horizon. Over millennia they created in this northern valley a civilization that rivaled the more famous ones (more famous thanks to Spanish chroniclers and gold) of the Aztecs, Mayas, and Incas farther south. Their great earthen fortifications, temple plazas, and tombs, along with the jewelry, carvings, and tools they buried with their dead, speak of complex and sophisticated cultures. From shells and flints and other materials found in their villages, we know their trade networks extended north beyond the Great Lakes, south to the Gulf of Mexico, east to the Atlantic, and west to the desert. Known collectively (and crudely) as the Mound Builders because of their impressive earthworks, these primordial settlers flourished along the Ohio from at least 1000 B.C. until roughly 1500 A.D., dates that encompass the golden age of Greece as well as the lifespans of the Assyrian, Persian, Roman, and Byzantine Empires.

When I was growing up in Ohio, where these industrious people left more than ten thousand mounds, I suspected every hillock of hiding skeletons decked out in bracelets of bear's teeth and necklaces of freshwater pearls. Although I walked the creek beds and farm fields with head bowed, on the lookout for arrowheads, some primitive awe kept me from digging into these humps of earth. But others were not so shy—after all, why respect the graves of heathens?—and gradually cupboards and museum shelves filled with the leavings of these vanished tribes.

What did the Ohio mean to the Mound Builders? The early white settlers, who rifled the tombs and leveled earthworks to clear the way for plows, did not care; and now it is too late for us to know for sure. But I would guess that the river was a god to them, a brawny presence, a strong back to ride through the forest, a giver of fish and mussels, flowing always and flooding when it took a notion. If you look at the most stunning of all the earthworks, the sinuous, quarter-mile-long Great Serpent Mound in southern Ohio, with its coiled tail and gaping mouth, and then look at the twisty Ohio itself, you can see that the river is a snake, the snake a river. In many mythologies, and even in the cellars of our own postmythic minds, the serpent is the raw intimidating power of nature itself, the pure energy of creation and destruction made visible. My hunch is that the Mound Builders felt this, worshipping the brown sinewy god and placing their villages on high ground to give the serpent room for writhing. If you are going to survive in the land, if you are ever going to be at home, you must know and honor the local powers, and nothing in this region is more steadily, undeniably powerful than the river.

No one knows what happened to the Mound Builders. They may have perished from epidemics or warfare, may have been forced out of the region by invaders or by their own overpopulation, or may have lived on to become one of the peoples known to history, such as the Shawnee. In any event, by the time Europeans reached the Ohio, the ceremonial earthworks had been abandoned. The valley was thinly settled by tribes that relied on hunting, fishing, the gathering of seeds and nuts, and the cultivation of corn, beans, and squash. Because the Ohio was prone to flood, these people built most of their villages on the tributaries instead of the main channel. In the eighteenth century, when traders and soldiers were filtering into the valley, the principal tribes included the powerful Iroquois north and east of the Forks of the Ohio, the Delaware and Wyandot along the Muskingum, the Shawnee on the Scioto, the Miami on the twin rivers that bear their name and on the Wabash, the Illinois on the Illinois, the Cherokee and Chickasaw on the Tennessee and Cumberland.

On a steamboat trip down the Ohio in 1841, Charles Dickens met a Choctaw chief who presented him with a calling card and then conversed with him, in English, about the poetry of Sir Walter Scott. Describing the incident in *American Notes for General Circulation*, Dickens clearly intended for his readers to lift their eyebrows at the spectacle of a savage become civilized. By 1841, however, the "savages" had maintained a civilization in the Ohio valley for several thousand years, far longer than descendants of Europeans and Africans have yet managed to survive here. If, say in the year 5000, *our* descendants are still living beside the Ohio in peace and prosperity, without having exhausted the soil or poisoned the river, then there will be cause for boasting. For now, we are still sojourners in the land, our wisdom untested, the durability of our ways unproved.

A good deal of ugly frontier history is compressed into one stanza of an early folk song about the river, preserved by Richard E. Banta in *The Ohio*

> *Those blood thirsty Indians you need not fear,*
> *We will all united be and we will be free from care,*
> *We'll march into their towns and give them their*
>   *deadly blow,*
> *And we'll fold you in our arms in the pleasant*
>   *Ohio.*

Native presence along the Ohio effectively came to an end in the mid-nineteenth century, when the Miami and Shawnee withdrew to the west. Before leaving, the Shawnee performed their sacred dances one last time, then covered the graves of their ancestors with grass. We can gain a sense of what these people might have thought about the river from an Iroquois creation myth, which tells how, in the beginning, the muskrat brought mud between its paws to Manitou, who lives in the river beneath the great falls. Manitou took the mud and made Earth. As Earth cooled, it took the shape of a pumpkin, and all creatures grew upon it. Waters ran down the valleys of the pumpkin and became rivers. Where the Iroquois traveled to fight their enemies and to kill buffalo and deer, the river was called the beautiful one, Ohio.

Anyone who has seen the river in flood can understand how the gathering of mud from the deeps and the emergence of land above the waters might stand for the mystery of creation itself.

Thanks in part to the Iroquois, who cleared out rival tribes from the upper Ohio, when the French and English entered the valley they found a sparsely settled land for the taking. And of course they took. What else was wilderness for? The name of the river itself was adopted and probably garbled from an Iroquois word, something like "Oyo," which the French translated as "beautiful river," but which later authorities have rendered as "great white water," "river of the white foam," or "bloody river." There is truth in all the names, even the claim of whitecaps, for the water is sometimes whipped into froth by the prevailing westerly winds.

Authorities also disagree about which European "discovered" the Ohio. Most say the honor goes to René-Robert Cavelier, Sieur de La Salle, who is supposed to have paddled downstream along with a Seneca guide and two dozen voyageurs as far as the falls in the winter of 1669–70; others say no, he never made the trip. No indisputable record of the journey has turned up. La Salle certainly *wanted* to find the river, for he believed it led to the western sea, and thence to the Orient and riches. He was so intent upon finding a quick route to the Far East that comrades named his Canadian estate "La Chine." Like many who followed him, he saw this region not as a place to be known and respected for its own sake, but as a pathway to somewhere more profitable. Trapping beaver as he went, he paid his bills with furs.

Whatever the truth of La Salle's claim, white hunters and traders and scalawags were visiting the river well before 1700, some venturing out from the French settlements on the Mississippi, others crossing the mountains from the English colonies. Identifying which of these Europeans first laid eyes on the Ohio, and when, has never seemed a burning question to me. The river was in no need of discovery, since the native people already knew where it was.

The question mattered a great deal to France and England, however. They spent a century feuding over who owned the river. One of the most revealing episodes in this long tussle occurred in 1749, when a

French captain named Céleron de Bienville deposited in the mouths of several tributaries engraved lead plates, which announced that the Ohio and all the streams flowing into it and all the uncharted lands drained by those waters belonged to King Louis XV. It was a brazen gesture, akin to planting a flag on the moon. With a handful of words, a potentate who had never so much as glimpsed North America laid claim to a realm that was nearly as large as his entire kingdom.

Although bewildered by the European notion of owning a river, the Iroquois and other tribes understood that forts and farms and log cabins were a threat to their own use of the land. During the eighteenth century, their rallying cry was, "White man shall not plant corn north of the Ohio." Partly to mollify these tribes, partly to confine the colonists within a more easily patrolled region, the British government, by a proclamation of 1763, forbade settlements west of the Appalachian Mountains. It was a decree widely ignored, even before the Revolution annulled all British proclamations. Families in search of land, investors eager for profit, and scamps fleeing debts or crimes or foul reputations, all looked eagerly toward the Ohio valley.

Among the first observers to record their impressions of the river were English commercial scouts. As an agent for the Ohio Land Company of Virginia, Christopher Gist explored the valley in 1750–1751, noting soils, timber, minerals, game, and the mood of the natives. Below the mouth of the Great Miami, he noticed

> fine, rich level Land, well timbered with large Wal-
> nut, Ash, Sugar Trees, Cherry Trees, &c, it is well
> watered with a great Number of little Streams or
> Rivulets, and full of beautiful natural Meadows,
> covered with Wild Rye, blue Grass and Clover, and
> abounds with Turkeys, Deer, Elks and most Sorts
> of Game particularly Buffaloes, thirty or forty of
> which are frequently seen feeding in one Meadow:
> In short it wants Nothing but Cultivation to make
> it a most delightfull Country.

That closing note was struck repeatedly in early accounts of the valley: here was a raw abundance need-
ing only shrewd investment and determined labor in
order to be turned into wealth.

As another example of the proprietary outlook,
consider George Washington's traffic with the Ohio.
While still a teenager, he surveyed land near the forks
at the behest of an English lord. The same year in
which Céleron deposited his lead plates, two of Washington's brothers helped form a company to colonize
the Ohio Valley. Soon after, Washington visited the
French troops near the headwaters, warning them in
the name of the Governor of Virginia to abandon their
fort and yield all claims to the river. The French
scoffed, war broke out, and Washington led troops
into battle for control of the valley. When at length the
British won, the king gave Washington five thousand
acres on the Ohio as a reward for his services. In a letter
of 1770 to Jefferson, Washington suggested opening a
path between the Potomac and the Ohio, to provide a
"channel of conveyance of the extensive and valuable
trade of a rising empire." He kept adding to his hold-

ings until, by the Revolution, he was one of the grandest landowners in the western country, amassing some sixty thousand acres. His real estate, plus his ambitions for the new nation, led him to keep pushing, after the Revolution, for the settlement of the Ohio country.

How did Washington see the river? Reading the journal from a trip he made downstream in 1770, we find ourselves in the company of a shrewd-eyed speculator. He assessed the fertility of bottomlands ("in many places very rich, in others somewhat wet and pondy; fit for meadow, but upon the whole exceeding valuable, as the land after you get out of the rich bottom is very good for grain"); the likely yield of meat ("This country abounds in buffaloes and wild game of all kinds; as also in all kinds of wild fowl, there being in the bottoms a great many small, grassy ponds, or lakes, which are full of swans, geese, and ducks"); the convenience of navigation ("When the river is in its natural state, large canoes, that will carry five or six thousand weight or more, may be worked against stream by four hands, twenty or twenty-five miles a day; and down, a good deal more"); and the disposition of the natives ("The Indians who reside upon the Ohio . . . view the settlement of the people upon this river with an uneasy and jealous eye"). In 1773 he placed an ad in a Baltimore paper for homesteads on the Ohio, a place "abounding with fine fish and wild fowl of various kinds, as also in most excellent meadows, in their present state, almost fit for the scythe."

The buying and selling of this vast new territory was made easier by the comprehensive survey mandated by the Ordinance of 1785. All land north of the river was divided into 640-acre, mile-square parcels, with the sides of the squares running north-south and east-west, a mathematical grid that would have pleased Sir Isaac Newton. The Northwest Ordinance of 1787 had an even more profound influence on the region, providing for the creation of new states and prohibiting slavery north of the river. That ban would make the Ohio a symbol of freedom for slaves escaping from the South; it would dot the northern shore with stops on the Underground Railroad; and, three-quarters of a century after passage of the Ordinance, the ban on slavery would make the river a highway for troops and supplies during the Civil War.

One of the drafters of the Northwest Ordinance was the Rev. Manasseh Cutler, who also wrote a description of the valley as it appeared to him in 1787:

> Besides the opportunity of opening a new and unexplored region for the range of natural history, botany, and the medical sciences, there will be one advantage which no other part of the earth can boast, and which probably will never again occur—that, in order to begin *right*, there will be no *wrong* habits to combat, and no inveterate systems to overturn—there is no rubbish to remove, before you can lay the foundation.

Like a new Eden, the valley of the Ohio offered natural bounty and the chance of a fresh start.

Early observers marveled over that plenitude. "The country hereabouts abounds with buffalo, bears, deer, and all sorts of wild game, in such plenty, that we killed out of our boats as much as we wanted," wrote George Croghan in 1765. Voyagers were still killing as much as they wanted half a century later, according to John James Audubon, who lived beside the Ohio for a dozen years: "The margins of the shores and of the river were . . . amply supplied with game. A Wild Turkey, a Grouse, or a Blue-winged Teal, could be procured in a few moments." In 1807, a traveler who relished the sight of eagles circling overhead noted that in one season a hunter killed two hundred deer and eighty bears. There were panthers and wildcats, fox and lynx, otters and minks, herds of elk, packs of wolves, whooping cranes by the flock, ducks and geese and partridges and pheasants by the skyful.

Well into the nineteenth century, it was common for travelers to see large animals swimming across the river. Here, for example, is an encounter from 1820: "Near midnight . . . we discovered something near us, which we took for a log, and began pulling from it, when we found our mistake; it was a bear swimming in the river; he came close to that part of the boat where I was standing, and then made off up the river in great haste. We could hear him blow in the water longer than we could see him." Boat passengers watched otters sliding on the banks, or beavers and muskrats churning in the shallows, or deer with gleaming antlers and frightened eyes wedging the current. Migrating squirrels crossed the water in such numbers that they formed thick gray rafts, blocking traffic.

More than a hundred species of fish lived in that un-polluted river, including bass, crappie, sturgeon, sunfish, rockfish, and several varieties of catfish—mud cats, channel cats, Mississippi blues—as well as mullet, perch, and carp. Even allowing for the exaggeration of fish stories, the size of some catches was astounding. Audubon reported that a friend hauled from the river near Louisville a catfish "in which was found the greater part of a sucking pig." Further downriver, near Henderson, Kentucky, using trotlines baited with toads, Audubon himself landed catfish weighing up to a hundred pounds. Frogs, turkey, the entrails of venison, any bait would do, the fish were so plentiful. Settlers could gather enough for their own tables using nets, or they could wade into the river at night carrying torches of pine knots or hickory bark and spear enough to feed the neighbors and the hogs as well.

Grapevines, heavy with fruit in season, laced tree to tree along the banks, and mistletoe clotted the branches. Sometimes a tree, chopped through at the base, would be held upright by the entangling vines. Where the river admitted sunlight to the forest floor, the undergrowth was so dense it made the shores almost impassable. Those uncut shores were lined with beech, maple and oak, with ash and hickory (ideal for ax-handles), tulip poplar (cabin logs), locust and cedar (fence posts), sassafras (tea), elm and chestnut, cottonwood, buckeye, juniper, luminous dogwood, redbud and magnolia, fruiting persimmon and mulberry, lithe willows and the fat, gnarly, white-flecked sycamores.

Then as now, you could judge the fertility of the soil by the dominant species: walnut, maple, buckeye, elm, and papaw grew on the richest land; and on the poorest grew hickory and black and white oak. Avoid beech forests, George Washington advised, "as their roots spread over a large surface of ground and are hard to kill." Then as now, open ground would be swiftly reclaimed by red cedar, locust, and sumac. Then as now, wildflowers licked up like flames from the earth, trout-lilies and trillium, rosy columbine and fire pinks, celandine poppies and spring beauties, phlox, goldenrods, mullein, Solomon's seal—a dazzling array.

For settlers, the early years in this territory were often grim. The historian Francis Parkman captured something of the mood of that time and place in his sketch of the frontier:

> Buried in woods, the settler lived in an appalling loneliness. A low-browed cabin of logs, with moss stuffed in the chinks to keep out the wind, roof covered with sheets of bark, chimney of sticks and clay, and square holes closed by a shutter in place of windows; an unkempt matron, lean with hard work, and a brood of children with bare heads and tattered garments eked out by deerskin,—such was the home of the pioneer in the remoter and wilder districts . . . the forest was everywhere, rolled over hill and valley in billows of interminable green,—a leafy maze, a mystery of shade, a universal hiding-place, where murder might lurk unseen at its victim's side, and Nature seemed formed to nurse the mind with wild and dark imaginings.

In spite of the menacing woods, in spite of Indians and snakes and wolves, settlers poured into the valley, one great wave coming after the Revolution and another—washing over my own neighborhood here in southern Indiana—after the War of 1812. Songs wooed them:

> The land it is good my boys you need not to fear
> 'Tis a garden of Eden in North America:
> Come along my lads and we'll altogether go
> And we'll settle on the banks of the pleasant Ohio.

For Audubon, who moved in with that rush of immigrants, the most astonishing abundance was that of passenger pigeons. Riding horseback toward Louisville along the Kentucky shore in 1813, he tried counting the flocks as they passed overhead but gave up out of weariness. "The air was literally filled with Pigeons; the light of noon-day was obscured as by an eclipse; the dung fell in spots, not unlike melting flakes of snow; and the continued buzz of wings had a tendency to lull my senses to repose." When he reached Louisville, some fifty miles later, "The Pigeons were still passing in undiminished numbers, and continued to do so for three days in succession." The dung beneath their roosts was several inches deep, and stout trees broke under their weight.

Who would have imagined that such riches could be exhausted? After describing the wholesale slaughter of pigeons in the beech forests along the river—heaps larger than haystacks rolling away on wagons, boatloads floating to city markets, hogs devouring the leftovers—Audubon added that "Persons unacquainted with these birds might naturally conclude that such dreadful havock would soon put an end to the species. But I have satisfied myself, by long observation, that nothing but the gradual diminution of our forests can accomplish their decrease." He was only half right; while the felling of forests did contribute to the decline of the passenger pigeon, it was the "dreadful havock" wrought by hunters that pushed the bird to extinction.

The pattern of habitat destruction and relentless hunting has been repeated for species after species. Bison, whose wide traces offered routes through the woods for the first roads, were still counted in hundreds at salt licks near the river on the eve of the Revolution, and yet within a few years they had been killed off. The lynx, wildcat, panther, elk, otter, bear, and wolf disappeared from the region; the green parakeet vanished altogether. The whooping cranes dwindled almost to extinction, and so did the bald eagles. By 1900, coal slurry and oil slicks from wells and mines on the upper river had killed off untold species of fish.

The vigorous cane, a jointed grass that shot up over a dozen feet, with stalks as thick as your arm, once flourished along the banks, providing color as well as fodder all year long. Cramer noted that "from its evergreen foliage, it has a pleasant effect on the imagination, when all the surrounding vegetable matter is locked up in the winter's frost." And yet the cane was soon eradicated through burning, clearing, and overgrazing. Although you can still see log trucks and steaming piles of sawdust on the shore, especially in

West Virginia and Indiana, the old growth timber is gone. We replant only the fastest growing and most profitable varieties of trees, so that our new forests are puny imitations of the original ones. Like the old timber, most of the oil and gas and iron ore near the Ohio was used up within a century, a brief time in the life of a river or a civilization.

When I look at the filth along parts of the Ohio, when I consider the annihilation of forests and the disappearance of wildlife, I cannot agree that such brief profit justifies so much desolation. Since the earliest days, the river has been used as a dump, receiving offal from slaughterhouses, sewage from towns, manure from livestock pens, mash from breweries, waste from factories and mines. Little was done to control pollution of the Ohio until the last few decades, and we are still a long way from having cleaned up our mess. This, too, is part of the river's history, the tar and chemicals, the oil slicks, the squandering within a few generations of an unforeseen, unearned bounty.

Despite George Washington's optimism about the convenience of navigation, the natural Ohio was an imperfect highway. Over its 981 miles, the river dropped only 430 feet, an average of less than six inches a mile. In low water, it was so shallow in places that a child could wade across. It remained low in the dry months of summer and in winter before the snowmelt, rising high enough for ready passage only in the rainy months of spring and fall. Even in high water, sunken trees, rocks, sandbars, and the wrecks of earlier boats made travel hazardous. Drift ice was a problem most winters, and about once in every ten years the river froze solid.

If the river was to become a thoroughfare, something would have to be done about these nuisances, especially about the falls at Louisville. (Actually, the "falls" were a series of rapids tumbling over limestone ledges, dropping only twenty-odd feet in three miles.) There were schemes afoot to dig a canal past the falls as early as 1787, and by 1825 the Kentuckians were actually digging one. About the time that canal opened for traffic, in 1830, the Army Corps of Engineers began hauling out snags and wrecks, blasting troublesome rocks, and dredging channels all up and down the Ohio. They built stone "training dikes" to narrow and deepen the river. But still, boats could travel only in the high water of spring and fall. Why not build a series of locks and dams, backing up enough water to guarantee a year-round depth of six feet? And once you get six feet, why not go for nine?

This grandiose scheme, proposed in 1875, was only carried out in our own century, after the scare of World War I and the near breakdown of the railroads pried the necessary funding from Congress. When the nine-foot channel was opened in 1929, Herbert Hoover declared: "While I am proud to be the President who witnesses the apparent completion of its improvement, I have the belief that some day new inventions and new pressures of population will require its further development." He was right about the unrelenting pressures. Before long the original fifty-one dams were replaced by nineteen new ones, each fitted with locks and steel doors for opening and shutting the river.

It is easy to forget this when you sit on the bank and watch the splayed roots of a tree creep by, or when you drift downstream in a skiff, but the Ohio has become, in fact, a chain of lakes, a grand canal for barges. I could quote you tedious figures about tonnage shipped (more passes along the Ohio than through the Suez or Panama Canals), but my point is about the drive to "improve" the river. Most picture books about the Ohio feature human works—dams and locks, boats and barges, highways and railroads, power plants, canals, levees, bridges, docks.

With rare exceptions, those who have left us records of their thinking about the Ohio and its valley have seen it as the raw material for human shaping, as if the landscape did not truly exist until we came along to transform it. I give three examples from hundreds that might serve. First, a tourist in 1803:

> When we see the forest cleared of those enormous trees . . . we cannot help dwelling upon the industry and art of man, which by dint of toil and perseverance can change the desert into a fruitful field . . . when the silence of nature is succeeded by the buzz of employment, the congratulations of society, and the voice of joy.

Next, a minister in 1849 celebrating the newfangled train that hugged the shore:

What music for the forest is a railroad train! . . . We
dashed along through these forest scenes . . . intent
only upon our mission of progress, though it
should oblige us to cut down all the trees in the universe, disturb the repose of nature in her lair, and
quench the lights of heaven by the smoke of our
civilizing chimneys.

Last, a Kentucky Congressman speaking in 1900:

And I tell you that I am neither a prophet nor the
son of a prophet, but one of the results of this
movement of river improvement will be that along
the valley of the Ohio, God's Eden restored, will
spring up on this great canal when it is completed,
as it will be completed, the peer of any city in this
or any other country on the reeling earth.

One is left reeling along with the earth after plowing
through such booster rhetoric. Dizzying as it may be,
it goes to the heart of our relationship with the river,
and with the American land. It is a relationship
founded on *use* and *possession*. The wild valley was a
"desert" awaiting our activity, a silence awaiting our
noise, a botched attempt at Eden that we in our wisdom would perfect.

While engineers saw the Ohio as a problem in plumbing, and explorers and merchants saw it as a highway
to somewhere else, and politicians saw it as an avenue
for power, and speculators saw it as an investment,
there have always been others who looked at the river

and found that most intangible of commodities, fine scenery. Mapping the river in 1766, Thomas Hutchins admired how "The stillness of the current and a calm sunshine put a Trace on the Water, from which was reflected the most beautiful objects of simple nature, that I ever beheld." In his *Notes on the State of Virginia*, Thomas Jefferson declared that "The *Ohio* is the most beautiful river on earth." The author of *The Navigator* outdid even that tribute by describing the Ohio as "beyond all competition, the most beautiful river in the universe." Many others have echoed these sentiments. In fact, when you scan the volumes of purple prose, it seems that every traveler who could wield a pen must have written impressions of the Ohio.

Early European visitors generally praised the scenery while regretting that much of the valley was still so wild. "Often a mountain torrent comes pouring its silver tribute to the stream," the Englishwoman Frances Trollope wrote in 1832, "and were there occasionally a ruined abbey, or a feudal castle, to mix the romance of real life with that of nature, the Ohio would be perfect." Mountain torrents happen to be as scarce on the Ohio as feudal castles; yet no literary river could do without them, so Frances Trollope put them in. Her hasty gaze is less disturbing than her assumption that the life of nature is false, and only human life is "real." Dickens, chronicler of cities, was also uneasy in this raw country: "For miles, and miles, and miles, these solitudes are unbroken by any sign of human life or trace of human footstep; nor is anything seen to move about them but the blue jay, whose color is so bright, and yet so delicate, that it looks like a flying flower."

The river would be more appealing, a German traveler suggested in 1852,

> If someday the forest primeval which now crowds and shades it is cleared a bit more, if its hills are crowned with country homes, if its bush-covered islands are adorned by little white cabins, and if its side valleys are cleared for views into the distance— then . . . a total impression will be formed in the mind of the observer that will be inferior to that of our Rhine only because it lacks memories of historical significance.

Many visitors seemed eager to clear the shores. Washington complained that "the sides of the river were a good deal incommoded with old trees, which impeded our passage." Frances Trollope, as usual, minced no words: "I never found the slightest beauty in the forest scenery. Fallen trees in every possible stage of decay, and congeries of leaves that have been rotting since the flood, cover the ground and infect the air."

Even American travelers, who often praised the very wildness that troubled Europeans, could not look at the river for long without celebrating what humans had made of it. Thus Charles Hoffman, a New Yorker, wrote in 1835 that one's "first view of the lovely river of the west is worth a journey of a thousand miles," but he quickly added a tribute to the "deeds done upon its banks—the wild incidents and savage encounters of border story." And Walt Whitman, an enthusiast rarely disappointed by American landscape, found the Ohio less grand than its reputation:

Like as in many other matters, people who travel on the Ohio, (that most beautiful of words!) for the first time, will stand a chance of being somewhat disappointed. In poetry and romance, these rivers are talked of as though they were cleanly streams; but it is astonishing what a difference is made by the simple fact that they are always and altogether excessively muddy—mud, indeed, being the prevailing character both afloat and ashore.

Although the history of our dealings with the Ohio has been, for the most part, one long saga of "improvement," not everyone has felt easy about the triumph of human will over the river. Here for example is Audubon, writing in the 1830s about his impressions from a quarter of a century earlier:

When I . . . call back to my mind the grandeur and beauty of those almost uninhabited shores; when I picture to myself the dense and lofty summits of the forests, that everywhere spread along the hills and overhung the margins of the stream, unmolested by the axe of the settler; . . . when I see that no longer any aborigines are to be found there, and that the vast herds of Elk, Deer, and Buffaloes which once pastured on these hills, and in these valleys, making for themselves great roads to the several salt-springs, have ceased to exist; when I reflect that all this grand portion of our Union, instead of being in a state of nature, is now more or less covered with villages, farms, and towns, . . . I pause, wonder, and although I know all to be fact, can scarcely believe its reality.

"Whether these changes are for the better or for the worse," Audubon mused, "I shall not pretend to say."

No one can escape this doubleness of vision. The river we see today is in part the offspring of glaciers and a million rains, in part our own creation. I feel closest to the primal river at dawn or dusk, when twilight erases our handiwork, or in fog, when the hills wear white rags and the water slides by, arriving from a mystery and vanishing into a fullness and confusion of light.

I still try to dig down through all our inherited images of the Ohio—as real estate, as highway, as plumbing, as scenery—to the river-in-itself. The Ohio can still speak to us of the holy, the nonhuman, as it spoke to the Mound Builders a millennium ago. What I feel when I ride on the water in a canoe or sit on the bank with my bare feet dangling, and I forget the dams, and I put the human buzz of barges and trucks and trains out of mind, is that the force driving the river also drives me. I do not mean simply gravity, but the whole thrust of the world that heaves us into existence and then draws us back to the source.

The river's movement is an outward show of the current that bears everything along. Wearing a groove in the earth, it reveals the grain of the universe. Quick or sluggish, all creation is a flow—rivers, mountains, trees, babies and parents, butterflies and parrots, rocks, clouds, sun, Milky Way—each part driven at its own pace within a single current. When I look in the mirror each morning the face I see is familiar from the day before, yet subtly changed, shifted downstream, as the river sliding within its banks alters moment by moment.

"And how I loved water," Theodore Roethke proclaimed in his notebook, "even a puddle shined with the face of the lord." Water is the medium of life. We are made of it, mostly. Our cells are tiny seas. Anyone who has held in the hand a freshly caught fish can see this streamlined shape as a bit of water with a temporary skin around it. So are we all. Near the river, you are reminded that water is the fundamental element on the surface of our planet; land is a latecomer and everywhere vulnerable. The mountains are hustling, grain by grain, toward the oceans. Near the river, you see water in its metamorphoses: as liquid, as fog and steam, as ice and snow, the endless cycling of stuff through its many forms. Near the river you are never far from an awareness of time, vast and moody and inhuman. Is time an arrow or a loop? The river dissolves that puzzle, for it is both arrow and loop, a current that moves in a circle, from hills to sea and back through snow and rain to hills, and so on down again to the sea. Perhaps our lives are segments in such a larger circle. Just as we are born from a sack of waters, so, in our stories, we cross a river—Lethe, Styx, Jordan—after death.

The Ohio carries for me the lights of the sky and the colors of the shore. It is the marriage of earth and air. Even in its chastened, diminished state, it holds out the promise of abundance, cleansing, and renewal. In fall, the maples along the banks still light their torches. In spring, the new leaves flare like struck matches. Viewed in the long perspective of ecology or in the briefer perspective of the merely human future, issues of ownership and profit seem trivial. What matters is the durability of land and water, how they bear up under our use.

If Audubon were to come back and have a look at the Ohio today, he might be able to make up his mind whether our tinkering with the river has been for the better or the worse. Without wanting to undo all of our work, I would relish a bit more wildness. Now that the shores have been cleared, I would trade a thousand acres of parking lots for a single acre of "forest primeval," with cane growing thicker than teeth on the river's edge, grapevines snarling the treetops a hundred feet in the air, larkspur flaming among the roots, brilliant green parakeets in the limbs, flocks of pigeons spiraling down to roost, bears pawing the rotten logs for grubs, and sycamores fatter than silos. I have nothing against hogs, but I would swap a herd of them for a single unpastured bison, would swap a train load for a woolly mammoth. And since I don't ship coal or sail a yacht, I would be glad to do without the dams; failing that, I would be satisfied if the engineers were to open the gates once a month or so and let the river flow.

Riverness—the appeal of a river, the way it speaks to us—has to do with our craving for a sense of direction within the seeming randomness of the world. Narrative offers us the same pleasure, a shape and direction imposed on time. And so we tell stories and listen to them as we listen to the coursing of water.

One night I was telling my children stories about

the Ohio. We were in Cincinnati's riverfront park, sitting on the curved, stairstepped levee they call the serpentine wall. It is the right shape for the river, the shape of the snaky brown god. I am glad the wall is there, a wise and handsome creation, a sign of what we can do when we have our wits about us. Tires whined overhead on the meshwork of a bridge, the same one from which, as a boy of five, I had first glimpsed the Ohio. Behind us, kids waded squealing in fountains and in front of us a dozen roaring boats crisscrossed the river.

Eva and Jesse had heard the stories before, but they indulged me by pretending every word was news. I told them how the tusks of mammoths discovered at Big Bone Lick were ground up to make fertilizer. I told them about river catfish weighing more than the anglers who caught them, about hollow sycamores large enough to shelter families, about floods that lifted cows through the second-story windows of a Louisville hotel. I told them how, in the days before sonar and radar, travelers estimated their distance from shore in darkness or fog by heaving stones and listening for the splash or thud. I told them how the northern shore, the shore where we made our home, had been known for a century as the Indian side, and how slaves crossed the river by night on their way to freedom, and how steamships raced with their safety valves tied down, and how pirates infested the cliffs in Illinois, and how in spring the thawing ice grumbled like cannon fire. I rattled on because I wanted my children to grow up carrying the Ohio in their minds.

Then after a while I realized that, like the tourists

and speculators, I was not speaking of the river but of us two-legged wonders. So I shut up. And as the darkness thickened, traffic thinned on the bridge. Boats put in for shore. The fountains stopped sputtering and the waders went home. Eventually there came a moment when the only sound was the shudder of the great muscular dragon body slithering in its bed. And that was the truest speech about the river.

CHAPTER FIVE

SETTLING DOWN

TWO FRIENDS ARRIVED AT
our house for supper one May evening along with the
first rumblings of thunder. As Ruth and I sat talking
with them on our front porch, we had to keep raising
our voices a notch to make ourselves heard above the
gathering storm. The birds, more discreet, had already hushed. The huge elm beside our door began to
sway, limbs creaking, leaves hissing. Black sponges of
clouds blotted up the light, fooling the street lamps
into coming on early. Above the trees and rooftops,
the murky southern sky crackled with lightning. Now
and again we heard the pop of a transformer as a bolt
struck the power lines in our neighborhood. The
pulses of thunder came faster and faster, until they
merged into a continuous roar.

We gave up on talking. The four of us, all Midwesterners teethed on thunderstorms, sat down there on the porch to our meal of lentil soup, cheddar cheese, bread warm from the oven, sliced apples and strawberries. We were lifting the first spoonfuls to our mouths when a stroke of lightning burst so nearby that it seemed to suck away the air, and the lights flickered out, plunging the whole street into darkness.

After we had caught our breath, we laughed—respectfully, as one might laugh at the joke of a giant. The sharp smell of ozone and the musty smell of damp earth mingled with the aroma of bread. A chill of pleasure ran up my spine. I lit a pair of candles on the table, and the flames rocked in the gusts of wind.

In the time it took for butter to melt on a slice of bread, the wind fell away, the elm stopped thrashing, the lightning let up, and the thunder ceased. The sudden stillness was more exciting than the earlier racket. A smoldering yellow light came into the sky, as though the humid air had caught fire. We gazed at one another over the steady candle flames and knew without exchanging a word what this eerie lull could mean.

"Maybe we should go into the basement," Ruth suggested.

"And leave this good meal?" one of our friends replied.

The wail of a siren broke the stillness—not the lesser cry of ambulance or fire engine or squad car, but the banshee howl of the civil defense siren at the park a few blocks away.

"They must have sighted one," I said.

"We could take the food down with us on a tray," Ruth told our guests.

"It's up to you," I told them. "We can go to the basement like sensible people, or we can sit here like fools and risk our necks."

"What do you want to do?" one of them asked me.

"You're the guests."

"You're the hosts."

"I'd like to stay here and see what comes," I told them.

Ruth frowned at me, but there we stayed, savoring our food and the sulphurous light. Eventually the siren quit. When my ears stopped ringing, I could hear the rushing of a great wind, like the whoosh of a waterfall. An utter calm stole over me. The hair on my neck bristled. My nostrils flared. Heat rose in my face as though the tip of a wing had raked over it.

Although I found myself, minutes later, still in the chair, the faces of my wife and friends gleaming in the candlelight, for a spell I rode the wind, dissolved into it, and there was only the great wind, rushing.

The tornado missed us by half a mile. It did not kill anyone in our vicinity, but it ripped off chimneys, toyed with cars, and plucked up a fat old maple by the roots.

Prudent folks would have gone to the basement. I do not recommend our decision; I merely report it. Why the others tarried on the porch I cannot say, but what kept me there was a mixture of curiosity and awe. I had never seen the whirling black funnel except in cautionary films, where it left a wake of havoc and tears. And now here was that tremendous power, paying us a visit. When a god comes calling, no matter how bad its reputation, would you go hide? If the siren had announced the sighting of a dragon, I would have sat there just the same, hoping to catch a glimpse of the spiked tail or fiery breath.

As a boy in Ohio I knew a farm family, the Millers, who not only saw but suffered from three tornadoes. The father, mother, and two sons were pulling into their driveway after church when the first tornado hoisted up their mobile home, spun it around, and carried it off. With the insurance money, they built a small frame house on the same spot. Several years later, a second tornado peeled off the roof, splintered the garage, and rustled two cows. The younger of the sons, who was in my class at school, told me that he had watched from the barn as the twister passed through, "And it never even mussed up my hair." The Millers rebuilt again, raising a new garage on the old foundation and adding another story to the house. That upper floor was reduced to kindling by a third tornado, which also pulled out half the apple trees and slurped water from the stock pond. Soon after that I left Ohio, snatched away by college as forcefully as by any cyclone. Last thing I heard, the family was preparing to rebuild yet again.

Why did the Millers refuse to budge? I knew them well enough to say they were neither stupid nor crazy. After the garage disappeared, the father hung a sign from the mailbox that read: TORNADO ALLEY. He figured the local terrain would coax future whirlwinds in their direction. Then why not move? Plain stubbornness was a factor. These were people who, once settled, might have remained at the foot of a volcano or on the bank of a flood-prone river or beside an earthquake fault. They had relatives nearby, helpful neighbors, jobs and stores and school within a short drive, and those were all good reasons to stay. But the main reason, I believe, was because the Millers had invested so much of their lives in the land, planting orchards and gardens, spreading manure on the fields, digging ponds, building sheds, seeding pastures. Out back of the house were groves of walnuts, hickories, and oaks, all started by hand from acorns and nuts. Honeybees zipped out from a row of white hives to nuzzle clover in the pasture. April through October, perennial flowers in the yard pumped out a fountain of blossoms. This farm was not just so many acres of dirt, easily exchanged for an equal amount elsewhere; it was a particular place, intimately known, worked on, dreamed over, cherished.

Psychologists tell us that we answer trouble with one of two impulses, either fight or flight. I believe that the Millers' response to tornadoes and my own keen expectancy on the porch arose from a third instinct, that of staying put. When the pain of leaving behind what we know outweighs the pain of embracing it, or when the power we face is overwhelming and neither fight nor flight will save us, there may be salvation in sitting still. And if salvation is impossible, then at least before perishing we may gain a clearer vision of where we are. By sitting still I do not mean the paralysis of dread, like that of a rabbit frozen beneath the dive of a hawk. I mean something like reverence, a respectful waiting, a deep attentiveness to forces much greater than our own. If indulged only for a moment, as in my case on the porch, this reverent impulse may amount to little; but if sustained for months and years, as by the Millers on their farm, it may yield marvels. The Millers knew better than to fight a tornado, and they chose not to flee. Instead they devoted themselves, season after season, to patient labor. Instead of withdrawing, they gave themselves more fully. Their commitment to the place may have been foolhardy, but it was also grand. I suspect that most human achievements worth admiring are the result of such devotion.

These tornado memories dramatize a choice we are faced with constantly: whether to go or stay, whether to move to a situation that is safer, richer, easier, more attractive, or to stick where we are and make what we can of it. If the shine goes off our marriage, our house, our car, do we trade it for a new one? If the fertility leaches out of our soil, the creativity out of our job, the money out of our pocket, do we start over somewhere else? There are voices enough, both inner and outer, urging us to deal with difficulties by pulling up stakes and heading for new territory. I know them well, for they have been calling to me all my days. I wish to raise here a contrary voice, to say a few words on behalf of standing your ground, confronting the powers, going deeper.

In a poem written not long before he leapt from a bridge over the Mississippi River, John Berryman ridiculed those who asked about his "roots" ("as if I were a *plant*"), and he articulated something like a credo for the dogma of rootlessness:

> *Exile is in our time like blood. Depend on*
> *interior journeys taken anywhere.*
>
> *I'd rather live in Venice or Kyoto,*
> *except for the languages, but*
> *O really I don't care where I live or have lived.*
> *Wherever I am, young Sir, my wits about me,*
>
> *memory blazing, I'll cope & make do.*

It is a bold claim, but also a hazardous one. For all his wits, Berryman in the end failed to cope well enough to stave off suicide. The truth is, none of us can live by wits alone. For even the barest existence, we depend on the labors of other people, the fruits of the earth, the inherited goods of our given place. If our interior journeys are cut loose entirely from that place, then both we and the neighborhood will suffer.

Exile usually suggests banishment, a forced departure from one's homeland. Famines and tyrants and wars do indeed force entire populations to flee; but most people who move, especially within the industrialized world, do so by choice. Salman Rushdie chose to leave his native India for England, where he has written a series of brilliant books from the perspective of a cultural immigrant. Like many writers, he has taken his own condition to represent not merely a possibility but a norm. In the essays of *Imaginary Homelands* he celebrates "the migrant sensibility," whose development he regards as "one of the central themes of this century of displaced persons." Rushdie has also taken this condition to represent something novel in history:

> The effect of mass migrations has been the creation of radically new types of human being: people who root themselves in ideas rather than places, in memories as much as in material things; people who have been obliged to define themselves—because they are so defined by others—by their otherness; people in whose deepest selves strange fusions occur, unprecedented unions between what they were and where they find themselves.

In the history of America, that description applies just as well to the Pilgrims in Plymouth, say, or to Swiss homesteading in Indiana, to Chinese trading in California, to former slaves crowding into cities on the Great Lakes, or to Seminoles driven onto reservations a thousand miles from their traditional land. Displaced persons are abundant in our century, but hardly a novelty.

Claims for the virtues of shifting ground are familiar and seductive to Americans, this nation of restless movers. From the beginning, our heroes have been sailors, explorers, cowboys, prospectors, speculators, backwoods ramblers, rainbow-chasers, vagabonds of every stripe. Our Promised Land has always been over the next ridge or at the end of the trail, never under our feet. One hundred years after the official closing of the frontier, we have still not shaken off the romance of unlimited space. If we fish out a stream or wear out a field, or if the smoke from a neighbor's chimney begins to crowd the sky, why, off we go to a new stream, a fresh field, a clean sky. In our national mythology, the worst fate is to be trapped on a farm, in a village, in the sticks, in some dead-end job or unglamorous marriage or played-out game. Stand still, we are warned, and you die. Americans have dug the most canals, laid the most rails, built the most roads and airports of any nation. In the newspaper I read that, even though our sprawling system of interstate highways is crumbling, the president has decided that we should triple it in size, and all without raising our taxes a nickel. Only a populace drunk on driving, a populace infatuated with the myth of the open road, could hear such a proposal without hooting.

So Americans are likely to share Rushdie's enthusiasm for migration, for the "hybridity, impurity, intermingling, the transformation that comes of new and unexpected combinations of human beings, cultures, ideas, politics, movies, songs." Everything about us is mongrel, from race to language, and we are stronger for it. Yet we might respond more skeptically when Rushdie says that "to be a migrant is, perhaps, to be the only species of human being free of the shackles of nationalism (to say nothing of its ugly sister, patriotism)." Lord knows we could do with less nationalism (to say nothing of its ugly siblings, racism, religious sectarianism, or class snobbery). But who would pretend that a history of migration has immunized the United States against bigotry? And even if, by uprooting ourselves, we shed our chauvinism, is that all we lose?

In this hemisphere, many of the worst abuses—of

land, forests, animals, and communities—have been carried out by "people who root themselves in ideas rather than places." Rushdie claims that "migrants must, of necessity, make a new imaginative relationship with the world, because of the loss of familiar habitats." But migrants often pack up their visions and values with the rest of their baggage and carry them along. The Spaniards devastated Central and South America by imposing on this New World the religion, economics, and politics of the Old. Colonists brought slavery with them to North America, along with smallpox and Norway rats. The Dust Bowl of the 1930s was caused not by drought but by the transfer onto the Great Plains of farming methods that were suitable to wetter regions. The habit of our industry and commerce has been to force identical schemes onto differing locales, as though the mind were a cookie-cutter and the land were dough.

I quarrel with Rushdie because he articulates as eloquently as anyone the orthodoxy that I wish to counter: the belief that movement is inherently good, staying put is bad; that uprooting brings tolerance, while rootedness breeds intolerance; that imaginary homelands are preferable to geographical ones; that to be modern, enlightened, fully of our time is to be displaced. Wholesale dis-placement may be inevitable; but we should not suppose that it occurs without disastrous consequences for the earth and for ourselves. People who root themselves in places are likelier to know and care for those places than are people who root themselves in ideas. When we cease to be migrants and become inhabitants, we might begin to pay enough heed and respect to where we are. By settling in, we have a chance of making a durable home for ourselves, our fellow creatures, and our descendants. /

What are we up against, those of us who aspire to become inhabitants, who wish to commit ourselves to a place? How strong, how old, is the impulse we are resisting?

Although our machines enable us to move faster and farther, humans have been on the move for a long time. Within a few clicks on the evolutionary clock, our ancestors roamed out of their native valleys in Africa and spread over the Eurasian continent. They invaded the deserts, the swamps, the mountains and valleys, the jungle and tundra. Drifting on boats and rafts, they pushed on to island after island around the globe. When glaciers locked up enough sea water to expose a land bridge from Asia to North America, migrants crossed into this unknown region, and within a few thousand years their descendants had scattered from the Bering Straits to Tierra del Fuego.

The mythology of those first Americans often claimed that a tribe had been attached to a given spot since the beginning of time, and we in our craving for rootedness may be inclined to believe in this eternal bond between people and place; but archaeology suggests that ideas, goods, and populations were in motion for millennia before the first Europeans reached these shores, hunters and traders and whole tribes roving about, boundaries shifting, homelands changing hands. Even agricultural settlements, such as those associated with the mound-building cultures in the Mississippi and Ohio valleys, reveal a history of arrivals and departures, sites used for decades or centuries and then abandoned. By comparison to our own hectic movements, an association between people and place lasting decades or centuries may seem durable and enviable; but it is not eternal.

What I am saying is that we are a wandering species, and have been since we reared up on our hind legs and stared at the horizon. Our impulse to wander, to pick up and move when things no longer suit us in our present place, is not an ailment brought on suddenly by industrialization, by science, or by the European hegemony over dark-skinned peoples. It would be naive to think that Spanish horses corrupted the Plains Indians, tempting a sedentary people to rush about, or that snowmobiles corrupted the Inuit, or that Jeeps corrupted the Aborigines. It would be just as naive to say that the automobile gave rise to our own restlessness; on the contrary, our restlessness gave rise to the automobile, as it led to the bicycle, steamboat, and clipper ship, as it led to the taming of horses, lacing of snowshoes, and carving of dugout canoes. With each invention, a means of moving farther, faster, has answered to a desire that coils in our genes. Mobility is the rule in human history, rootedness the exception.

Our itch to wander was the great theme of the English writer Bruce Chatwin, who died in 1989 from a rare disease contracted in the course of his own incessant travels. For Chatwin, "the nature of human restlessness" was "the question of questions." One hundred pages of *The Songlines*, his best known work, are filled with notebook entries supporting the view that "man is a migratory species." In a posthumous collection of essays entitled *What Am I Doing Here*, he summed up his observations:

> [W]e should perhaps allow human nature an appetitive drive for movement in the widest sense. The act of journeying contributes towards a sense of physical and mental well-being, while the monotony of prolonged settlement or regular work weaves patterns in the brain that engender fatigue and a sense of personal inadequacy. Much of what the ethologists have designated "aggression" is simply an angered response to the frustrations of confinement.

I am dubious about the psychology here, for I notice Chatwin's own frustrations in the passage, especially in that irritable phrase about "the monotony of prolonged settlement or regular work;" but I agree with his speculation that deep in us there is "an appetitive drive for movement."

The movement chronicled in *The Songlines*—the purposeful wandering of the Australian Aborigines—may suggest a way for us to harness our restlessness, a way to reconcile our need to rove with our need to settle down. As hunter-gatherers in a harsh continent, the Aborigines must know their land thoroughly and travel it widely in order to survive. According to their belief, the land and all living things were created in a mythic time called the Dreaming, and the creative spirits are still at work, sustaining the world. Humans keep the world in touch with the power of the Dreaming by telling stories and singing songs. The whole of

Australia is crisscrossed by pathways known to the Aborigines, who must walk them at intervals, performing the songs that belong to each path. Every tribe is responsible for the tracks within its own territory, and for passing down the appropriate songs from generation to generation. "There was hardly a rock or creek in the country," Chatwin remarks, "that could not or had not been sung." The movement of the Aborigines is not random, therefore, but deliberate, guided by hunger and thirst, but also by the need to participate in the renewal of the world. The land supplies the necessities of life, and in return humans offer knowledge, memory, and voice.

The Aboriginal walkabout illustrates "the once universal concept," in Chatwin's words, "that wandering re-establishes the original harmony . . . between man and the universe." Unlike vagabonds, who use up place after place without returning on their tracks, the Aborigines wed themselves to one place, and range over it with gratitude and care. So that they might continue as residents, they become stewards. Like the rest of nature, they move in circles, walking again and again over sacred ground.

The Australian Aborigines are among the "inhabitory peoples" whom Gary Snyder has studied in his search for wisdom about living in place, a wisdom he described in *The Old Ways*:

> People developed specific ways to *be* in each of those niches: plant knowledge, boats, dogs, traps, nets, fishing—the smaller animals, and smaller

tools. From steep jungle slopes of Southwest China to coral atolls to barren arctic deserts—*a spirit of what it was to be there* evolved, that spoke of a direct sense of relation to the "land"—which really means, the totality of the local bio-region system, from cirrus clouds to leaf-mold.

Such knowledge does not come all at once; it accumulates bit by bit over generations, each person adding to the common lore.

Even nomads, whose name implies motion, must be scholars of their bioregion. As they follow herds from pasture to pasture through the cycle of the year, they trace a loop that is dictated by what the land provides. For inhabitory peoples, listening to the land is a spiritual discipline as well as a practical one. The alertness that feeds the body also feeds the soul. In Native American culture, "medicine" is understood not as a human invention, but as a channeling of the power by which all things live. Whether you are a hunter-gatherer, a nomad, a farmer, or a suburbanite, to be at home in the land is to be sane and whole.

The Aborigines worked out an accommodation with their land over forty thousand years, no doubt through trial and error. They would not have survived if their mythology had not soon come to terms with their ecology. Even so, their population was never more than about one hundredth as large as that of modern Australia. We who live in North America are engaged in our own trials and errors, which are greatly magnified by the size of our population and the power of our technology. A man with a bulldozer can make a graver mistake in one day than a whole tribe with digging sticks can make in a year. In my home region, mistakes are being made seven days a week—with machinery, chemicals, guns, plows, fountain pens, bare hands. I suspect the same is true in every region. But who is keeping track? Who speaks for the wordless creatures? Who supplies memory and conscience for the land?

Half a century ago, in *A Sand County Almanac*, Aldo Leopold gave us an ecological standard for judging our actions: "A thing is right when it tends to preserve the integrity, stability, and beauty of the biotic community. It is wrong when it tends otherwise." We can only apply that standard if, in every biotic community, there are residents who keep watch over what is preserved and what is lost, who see the beauty that escapes the frame of the tourist's windshield or the investor's spreadsheet. "The problem," Leopold observed, "is how to bring about a striving for harmony with land among a people many of whom have forgotten there is any such thing as land, among whom education and culture have become almost synonymous with landlessness."

The question is not whether land belongs to us, through titles registered in a courthouse, but whether we belong to the land, through our loyalty and awareness. In the preface to his *The Natural History and Antiquities of Selborne*, the eighteenth-century English vicar, Gilbert White, notes that a comprehensive survey of England might be compiled if only "stationary men would pay some attention to the districts on which they reside." Every township, every field and creek, every mountain and forest on Earth would benefit from the attention of stationary men and women. No one has understood this need better than Gary Snyder:

> One of the key problems in American society now, it seems to me, is people's lack of commitment to any given place—which, again, is totally unnatural and outside of history. Neighborhoods are allowed to deteriorate, landscapes are allowed to be strip-mined, because there is nobody who will live there and take responsibility; they'll just move on. The reconstruction of a people and of a life in the United States depends in part on people, neighborhood by neighborhood, county by county, deciding to stick it out and make it work where they are, rather than flee.

We may not have forty years, let alone forty thousand, to reconcile our mythology with our ecology. If we are to reshape our way of thinking to fit the way of things, as the songs of the Aborigines follow their terrain, many more of us need to *know* our local ground, walk over it, care for it, fight for it, bear it steadily in mind.

But if you stick in one place, won't you become a stick-in-the-mud? If you stay put, won't you be narrow, backward, dull? You might. I have met ignorant people who never moved; and I have also met ignorant people who never stood still. Committing yourself to a place does not guarantee that you will become wise, but neither does it guarantee that you will become parochial. Who knows better the limitations of a province or a culture than the person who has bumped into them time and again? The history of settlement in my own district and the continuing abuse of land hereabouts provoke me to rage and grief. I know the human legacy here too well to glamorize it.

To become intimate with your home region, to know the territory as well as you can, to understand your life as woven into the local life does not prevent you from recognizing and honoring the diversity of other places, cultures, ways. On the contrary, how can you value other places if you do not have one of your own? If you are not yourself *placed*, then you wander the world like a sightseer, a collector of sensations, with no gauge for measuring what you see. Local knowledge is the grounding for global knowledge. Those who care about nothing beyond the confines of their parish are in truth parochial, and are at least mildly dangerous to their parish; on the other hand, those who *have* no parish, those who navigate ceaselessly among postal zones and area codes, those for whom the world is only a smear of highways and bank accounts and stores, are a danger not just to their parish but to the planet.

Since birth, my children have been surrounded by images of the earth as viewed from space, images that I first encountered when I was in my twenties. Those photographs show vividly what in our sanest moments we have always known—that the earth is a closed circle, lovely and rare. On the wall beside me as I write there is a poster of the big blue marble encased in its white swirl of clouds. That is one pole of my awareness; but the other pole is what I see through my window. I try to keep both in sight at once.

For all my convictions, I still have to wrestle with the fear—in myself, in my children, and in some of my neighbors—that our place is too remote from the action. This fear drives many people to pack their bags and move to some resort or burg they have seen on television, leaving behind what they learn to think of as the boondocks. I deal with my own unease by asking just what action I am remote *from*—a stock market? a debating chamber? a drive-in mortuary? The action that matters, the work of nature and community, goes on everywhere.

Since Copernicus we have known better than to see the earth as the center of the universe. Since Einstein, we have learned that there is no center; or alternatively, that any point is as good as any other for observing the world. I take this to be roughly what medieval theologians meant when they defined God as a circle whose circumference is nowhere and whose center is everywhere. I find a kindred lesson in the words of the Zen master, Thich Nhat Hanh: "This spot where you sit is your own spot. It is on this very spot and in this very moment that you can become enlightened. You don't have to sit beneath a special tree in a distant land." There are no privileged locations. If you stay put, your place may become a holy center, not because it gives you special access to the divine, but because in your stillness you hear what might be heard anywhere. All there is to see can be seen from anywhere in the universe, if you know how to look; and the influence of the entire universe converges on every spot.

Except for the rare patches of wilderness, every place on earth has been transformed by human presence. "Ecology becomes a more complex but far more interesting science," René Dubos observes in *The Wooing of Earth*, "when human aspirations are regarded as an integral part of the landscape." Through "long periods of intimate association between human beings and nature," Dubos argues, landscape may take on a "quality of blessedness." The intimacy is crucial: the understanding of how to dwell in a place arises out of a sustained conversation between people and land. When there is no conversation, when we act without listening, when we impose our desires without regard for the qualities or needs of our place, then landscape may be cursed rather than blessed by our presence.

If our fidelity to place is to help renew and preserve our neighborhoods, it will have to be informed by what Wendell Berry calls "an ecological intelligence: a sense of the impossibility of acting or living alone or solely in one's own behalf, and this rests in turn upon a sense of the order upon which any life depends and of the proprieties of place within that order." Proprieties of place: actions, words, and values that are *proper* to your home ground. I think of my home ground as a series of nested rings, with house and marriage and family at the center, surrounded by the wider and wider hoops of neighborhood and community, the bioregion within walking distance of my door, the wooded hills and karst landscape of southern Indiana, the watershed of the Ohio River, and so on outward—and inward—to the ultimate source.

The longing to become an inhabitant rather than a drifter sets me against the current of my culture, which nudges everyone into motion. Newton taught us that a body at rest tends to stay at rest, unless acted on by an outside force. We are acted on ceaselessly by outside forces—advertising, movies, magazines, speeches—and also by the inner force of biology. I am not immune to their pressure. Before settling in my present home, I lived in seven states and two countries, tugged from place to place in childhood by my father's work and in early adulthood by my own. This itinerant life is so common among the people I know that I have been slow to conceive of an alternative. Only by knocking against the golden calf of mobility, which looms so large and shines so brightly, have I come to realize that it is hollow. Like all idols, it distracts us from the true divinity.

The ecological argument for staying put may be easier for us to see than the spiritual one, worried as we are about saving our skins. Few of us worry about saving our souls, and fewer still imagine that the condition of our souls has anything to do with the condition of our neighborhoods. Talk about enlightenment makes us jittery because it implies that we pass our ordinary days in darkness. You recall the scene in *King Lear* when blind and wretched old Gloucester, wishing to commit suicide, begs a young man to lead him to the brink of a cliff. The young man is Gloucester's son, Edgar, who fools the old man into thinking they have come to a high bluff at the edge of the sea. Gloucester kneels, then tumbles forward onto the level ground; on landing, he is amazed to find himself alive. He is transformed by the fall. Blind, at last he is able to see his life clearly; despairing, he discovers hope. To be enlightened, he did not have to leap to someplace else; he only had to come hard against the ground where he already stood.

My friend Richard, who wears a white collar to his job, recently bought forty acres of land that had been worn out by the standard local regimen of chemicals and corn. Evenings and weekends, he has set about restoring the soil by spreading manure, planting clover and rye, and filling the eroded gullies with brush. His pond has gathered geese, his young orchard has tempted deer, and his nesting boxes have attracted swallows and bluebirds. Now he is preparing a field for the wildflowers and prairie grasses that once flourished here. Having contemplated this work since he was a boy, Richard will not be chased away by fashions or dollars or tornadoes. On a recent airplane trip he was distracted from the book he was reading by thoughts of renewing the land. So he sketched on the flyleaf a plan of labor for the next ten years. Most of us do not have forty acres to care for, but that should not keep us from sowing and tending local crops.

I think about Richard's ten-year vision when I read a report chronicling the habits of computer users who, apparently, grow impatient if they have to wait more than a second for their machine to respond. I use a computer, but I am wary of the haste it encourages.

Few answers that matter will come to us in a second; some of the most vital answers will not come in a decade, or a century.

When the chiefs of the Iroquois nation sit in council, they are sworn to consider how their decisions will affect their descendants seven generations into the future. Seven generations! Imagine our politicians thinking beyond the next opinion poll, beyond the next election, beyond their own lifetimes, two centuries ahead. Imagine our bankers, our corporate executives, our advertising moguls weighing their judgments on that scale. Looking seven generations into the future, could a developer pave another farm? Could a farmer spray another pound of poison? Could the captain of an oil tanker flush his tanks at sea? Could you or I write checks and throw switches without a much greater concern for what is bought and sold, what is burned?

As I write this, I hear the snarl of earthmovers and chain saws a mile away destroying a farm to make way for another shopping strip. I would rather hear a tornado, whose damage can be undone. The elderly woman who owned the farm had it listed in the National Register, then willed it to her daughters on condition they preserve it. After her death, the daughters, who live out of state, had the will broken, so the land could be turned over to the chain saws and earthmovers. The machines work around the clock. Their noise wakes me at midnight, at three in the morning, at dawn. The roaring abrades my dreams. The sound is a reminder that we are living in the midst of a holocaust. I do not use the word lightly. The earth is being pillaged, and every one of us, willingly or grudgingly, is taking part. We ask how sensible, educated, supposedly moral people could have tolerated slavery or the slaughter of Jews. Similar questions will be asked about us by our descendants, to whom we bequeath an impoverished planet. They will demand to know how we could have been party to such waste and ruin. They will have good reason to curse our memory.

What does it mean to be alive in an era when the earth is being devoured, and in a country which has set the pattern for that devouring? What are we called to do? I think we are called to the work of healing, both inner and outer: healing of the mind through a change in consciousness, healing of the earth through a change in our lives. We can begin that work by learning how to abide in a place. I am talking about an active commitment, not a passive lingering. If you stay with a husband or wife out of laziness rather than love, that is inertia, not marriage. If you stay put through cowardice rather than conviction, you will have no strength to act. Strength comes, healing comes, from aligning yourself with the grain of your place and answering to its needs.

"The man who is often thinking that it is better to be somewhere else than where he is excommunicates himself," we are cautioned by Thoreau, that notorious stay-at-home. The metaphor is religious: to withhold yourself from where you are is to be cut off from communion with the source. It has taken me half a lifetime of searching to realize that the likeliest path to the ultimate ground leads through my local ground. I mean the land itself, with its creeks and rivers, its weather, seasons, stone outcroppings, and all the plants and animals that share it. I cannot have a spiritual center without having a geographical one; I cannot live a grounded life without being grounded in a *place*.

In belonging to a landscape, one feels a rightness, at-homeness, a knitting of self and world. This condition of clarity and focus, this being fully present, is akin to what the Buddhists call mindfulness, what Christian contemplatives refer to as recollection, what Quakers call centering down. I am suspicious of any philosophy that would separate this-worldly from other-worldly commitment. There is only one world, and we participate in it here and now, in our flesh and our place.

CHAPTER SIX

GROUND NOTES

THE DIRT IN MY NEIGHBOR-
hood has begun to thaw, releasing a meaty, succulent
smell that is older than I am, older than humankind,
older than anything I can see from my window except
the sun and moon. The smell promises the resurrec-
tion of the year. Soon the brown blades of winter will
flicker with green. The purple buds of crocuses and the
white of bloodroot will pierce the leaf duff and open
their hinges to the bees.

This fecund smell breaks my clocks, spreading me
over all my ages at once, so that I am a toddler digging
in the spring dirt of a Tennessee cotton field, and I am
a boy staggering behind a plow in Ohio on the lookout
for arrowheads, and I am a teenager stalking muskrats
along a river that has not yet been dammed, and I am a

lone young man lured to the melancholy roar of the ocean on the coast of Rhode Island, and I am a husband and father here in Indiana transplanting ferns and fire pinks into my garden. Thawing dirt also breaks the grip of winter in me. The promise of new life in that loamy smell gives me courage to ask questions I have been afraid to ask.

What do I fear? A story is told of the physicist who, upon learning that matter is made up almost entirely of empty space, began wearing boots with enormous soles to keep himself from falling through the gaps. In cartoons, the hapless coyote races over the edge of a cliff and keeps on blithely running until he chances to look down, whereupon he plummets. I sympathize with coyote and physicist both. The void that opens beneath me is not the vacancy within atoms, nor the gulf of air, but the void of ignorance. I do not know where I am. I look down and cannot say what ground is beneath my feet.

The ignorance I am talking about stretches from the dirt to the stars, and even beyond the stars to the source of music for this cosmic dance. Consider that lowly dirt. The soil thawing outside my window contains humus from generations of decay, silt from glaciers which last visited these parts ten thousand years ago, clay from the decomposition of three-hundred-million-year-old limestone, and the debris from supernovas that exploded before the birth of our sun. A handful of that soil may contain a billion organisms, each one burning with life. I doubt that these myriad beasties are troubled by their ignorance of me, but how can I live without giving them thought? Yet if I opened my mind to even 1 percent of those creatures, would I have room for anything else?

Ignorance is bliss only so long as you do not know how little you know. In the Genesis account, on the third day the Creator divided water from dry land. Now there would be a place for the grass to grow, the grains to lift their seeds, the birds to make their nests, a place for the four-legged beasts to slink and run, a place for us two-legged animals to walk. All very comforting, so long as one believes—as the people who recorded the story did believe—that the land visible within the horizon's hoop is a large proportion of all there is. Very comforting, until one learns that land and sea stretch on and on beyond the horizon to form a globe, and this globe is but a speck in orbit around a run-of-the-mill star, and the star is caught in the outer arm of a spiral galaxy, and the galaxy itself is but a speck flung amid an untold dusting of other galaxies within a space whose outer limits we have not yet seen, and the space we see may be no more than one bubble in an ocean of universes. Who, grasping that, can avoid feeling vertigo?

I have had since childhood a recurrent dream, one of the commonest in the lexicon of dreams. I walk out along some high surface—an airplane wing in flight, the rim of a water tower, a windowsill on the top floor of a skyscraper. Unaware at first that a gulf opens beneath me, I move with assurance until, like the coyote, I glance down, and then I panic, lose my footing, and fall. As I tumble, I realize that I am dreaming, and that unless I wake before hitting the earth I will die. So far, I have always managed to claw my way up out of sleep.

Awake or asleep, one day I *will* die, of course. That knowledge darkens the shadows over which I balance. In my waking hours, I have the dizzying sense of looking down into the abyss whenever I ask where it is I actually live, and what this broody "I" might be that does the living, and how both place and self are bound to the rest of the world. What is my true home? Is there solid footing anywhere? If so, how can I reach it? If not, on what shall I stand?

These questions are the ground notes of my life, playing beneath everything I do, like the steady bass notes in Bach's music that underlie the surface melodies. They are also questions *about* the ground, a reaching toward the outermost circumference and innermost core of things.

Some years ago a utility company wanted to build a nuclear power plant on the sandy shore of Lake Michigan near Chicago. Their permit required them to set their foundations on bedrock, so down they drilled through the sand, down and down; but after excavating a very expensive hole, they still had not come to solid rock. Having made what they considered an honest effort, they petitioned the regulatory agency to allow them to anchor the foundations in a considerable depth of sand, and treat that as the equivalent of bedrock. The agency, to their credit (and to my surprise), said no. So the utility rolled up their blueprints and trudged back to the board room. But most of us, after failing in our own efforts to drill all the way to bed-rock, give up and build our lives on shifty sand.

Ground, *foundation*, and *fundamental* all derive from roots meaning *bottom*, as in, "I'll get to the bottom of this." But *is* there a bottom, and even if there is can we ever get down to it? "There is a solid bottom every where," Thoreau assures us in *Walden*. That cantankerous book is a prolonged invitation to dig:

> Let us settle ourselves, and work and wedge our feet downward through the mud and slush of opinion, and prejudice, and tradition, and delusion, and appearance, that alluvion which covers the globe, through Paris and London, through New York and Boston and Concord, through church and state, through poetry and philosophy and religion, till we come to a hard bottom and rocks in place, which we can call *reality*, and say, This is, and no mistake; and then begin.

I share his aspiration, but not his confidence. The aspiration is an old one. Twenty-five centuries before Thoreau, Lao-tzu wrote in the *Tao Te Ching*:

> By many words is wit exhausted.
> Rather, therefore, hold to the core.

Gladly: but how to find it, this core?

As a boy, I thought I might find the ultimate ground in the Bible. I studied the fine print with the urgency of a child lost in the labyrinth who is seeking the thread that will lead him home. With Job (38: 4–7), I heard the Lord roaring from the whirlwind:

> *Where were you when I laid the foundation of the*
> *earth?*
> *Tell me, if you have understanding.*
> *Who determined its measurements—surely you*
> *know!*
> *Or who stretched the line upon it?*
> *On what were its bases sunk,*
> *or who laid its cornerstone,*
> *when the morning stars sang together,*
> *and all the sons of God shouted for joy?*

After combing through the Bible, I scoured the holy texts of other religions. Everywhere I looked, I came across rumors of the primal power. In *The Upanishads*, for example:

> *Just as a spider spins forth its thread and draws it in*
> *again,*
> *The whole creation is woven from Brahman and*
> *unto It returns.*
> *Just as plants are rooted in the earth,*
> *All beings are supported by Brahman.*
> *Just as hair grows from a person's head,*
> *So does everything arise from Brahman.*

Or in the *Tao Te Ching*:

> *Before the Heaven and Earth existed*
> *There was something nebulous:*
> *Silent, isolated,*

Standing alone, changing not,
Eternally revolving without fail,
Worthy to be the Mother of All Things.
I do not know its name
And address it as Tao.

Eventually I realized that nobody knew its name. These holy texts could only gesture toward the source, whether they addressed it as Tao, Brahman, Yahweh or God, as Logos, Dharma, Atman, World Soul, Manitou, or Spirit Keeper. In scripture after scripture, the ground I was seeking slipped through the white spaces between words.

So then I searched in music, painting, and literature. I read shelves of poetry and fiction, Auden through Zola. I listened to Bach until my skull reverberated to his harmonics. I peered into Van Gogh's flaming sunflowers and starry nights until the air began to spark. But still there were gaps between notes, brush strokes, words. No screen was fine enough to catch the flow of reality, no frame large enough to contain it.

Next I tried science, beginning with biology, the squishiest of the hard sciences, then chemistry, that erector set of atoms and bonds, and finally physics, which pursues reality with the butterfly net of mathematics, the finest mesh of all. At least since Democritus speculated about atoms twenty-five centuries ago, scientists have been hunting for the ultimate building blocks and fundamental laws of matter. It is the same quest that Thoreau describes, a delving down through opinion and appearances to a "hard bottom," to *reality*. The scientific search, like the religious one, is inspired by a conviction that there *is* a ground, a single source underlying all the surface variety we see, and that we can apprehend it through the power of mind.

I remember encountering in freshman physics class the following simple and terrifying idea: Imagine all things spread out according to size upon a great ladder, with atoms and such minutiae toward the bottom, and galaxies and other giants toward the top, and humans somewhere in the middle. Moving up one rung on the ladder means jumping to a scale ten times as large, and moving down means decreasing to a scale one tenth as large. For simplicity, as the scientists like to say—and also perhaps for humility—let us begin not with ourselves, an awkward size, but with an animal that is a meter long: a collie, say. The step up from a collie would be a scale of ten meters, the length of a smallish whale, or, if you prefer, the height of a two-story house. Two rungs above the collie we would leave the range of animals entirely and reach the size of a football field. The next level would carry us to a thousand meters, roughly the length of three aircraft carriers placed end-to-end. Within only seven jumps of this sort we would rise to the diameter of the earth, and six more would carry us to that of the solar system, and so on rapidly up and up, beyond the scale of the Milky Way, then our local cluster of galaxies, then clusters of clusters, until our vision gives out somewhere in the neighborhood of twenty-five rungs above the collie.

Reverse directions, and the descent is equally precipitous. The step down from a collie would be one tenth of a meter, the size of a chickadee or a grapefruit. One more rung down and we reach the pesky house fly, the next lower and we come to the size of coarse sand. Again, after only a few more rungs, we fall below the scale of amoebas and bacteria, below the smallest microorganisms, into the domain of molecules, atoms, protons, electrons, quarks, until once more our vision gives out, roughly fifteen rungs beneath the collie.

From largest to smallest, the range over which we can presently see is about forty steps on the ladder. Whether going up or down, we eventually reach a level beyond which our instruments can no longer peer. How many levels there are, or whether they ever end, we do not know; and some theories—including a troublesome one propounded in mathematics by Kurt Gödel and the even more troubling uncertainty principle formulated by Werner Heisenberg—argue that in principle we *cannot* know. The farther out or the deeper in we look, the fainter and more ambiguous the information, and the greater the distortion imposed by our ways of looking. Heisenberg warned us "to remember that what we observe is not nature in itself but nature exposed to our method of questioning. Our scientific work in physics consists in asking questions about nature in the language that we possess and trying to get an answer from experiment by the means that are at our disposal."

The point is that we will never see to the outermost circumference or innermost core of things with eye or instrument alone. Physics is a grand endeavor, one I follow with a fan's enthusiasm, but not even the most powerful accelerator will ever knock on reality's hard bottom, not even the subtlest equation will perfectly map the universe. And even the superb maps that physics does provide ignore too much of what we know by other means. To say, for example, that you and I and your cat and my banjo are just so many piles of quarks may be true, but it misses some crucial distinctions.

If neither scripture nor art nor science can lay bare the primal ground, where do we set our feet? For all his crowing confidence, Thoreau himself was aware of the difficulty. In *Walden* he relates an anecdote about a traveler who comes to the edge of a swamp and asks a neighborhood boy if the swamp has a hard bottom. Sure does, the boy replies. So the traveler rides forward and his horse promptly sinks in up to the saddle girth. "I thought you said that this bog had a hard bottom," the man complains. "So it has," the boy answers, "but you have not got half way to it yet."

Note that in my example of the ladder I am talking about a hierarchy of size, not of importance. I do not mean to drag in the old notion of a chain of being, which would start down among the worms and ascend past us to the angels and beyond the angels to God. Even in the heyday of that notion, in the eighteenth century, the observant Gilbert White insisted that "Earth-worms, though in appearance a small and despicable link in the chain of Nature, yet, if lost, would make a lamentable chasm." I would extend White's claim to say that there are no despicable links; the loss of any life makes a chasm. Whatever divinity there is runs through every step on the ladder.

Mention of divinity will make some readers nervous. It makes *me* nervous. But I cannot avoid religious language. The root meaning of *religion* is to bind together. The only way to avoid being religious, in that original sense, is to pretend that the universe does not cohere. It does cohere, beautifully. On every scale we have been able to examine, from quarks to supergalactic clusters, we find structure. Even what we used to label chaos now appears to obey rules. In the history of science, every time we have come up against phenomena that seemed haphazard, they turned out to be lawful on a scale we had not yet grasped.

To insist that nature is orderly is not to say it is tidy, like a billiard ball, or easy to grasp, like a doorknob, or that it has been set up like a doll house for our little human play. In *Moby-Dick*, Melville's narrator speculates that the whiteness of the whale terrifies us because it is a reminder of "the heartless voids and immensities of the universe, and thus stabs us from behind with the thought of annihilation." He describes the blank forehead of Moby-Dick as an image of the "colorless, all-color of atheism from which we shrink." If the whale's whiteness fairly sums up the world, if reality is nothing but random collisions of particles, then the universe is absurd. For most of a century, it has been fashionable among intellectuals to say so. But not one of them could have stood upright, held a pen, or digested supper without participating in an exquisite and, for all we can see, infinite order.

Just because we cannot lay our fingers on the pulse, does not mean the universe is heartless. What presumption, to imagine that because we are bewildered the universe must be a muddle, or that because we cannot see a direction in things there must be no purpose. Even sober scientists have been known to project our uncertainties onto the cosmos. Steven Weinberg, a Nobel laureate in physics, concluded his account of the big bang with a sentence that sticks in the mind like a burr: "The more the universe seems comprehensible, the more it also seems pointless." Commenting on this passage in an interview, the cosmologist James Peebles said, reasonably enough, "I have never demanded that the universe explain to me why it's doing what it's doing."

My life, or any life, is a knot where an infinite number of threads lace together. Tease out one of those threads, trace it as far as you can, and eventually you come up against the unknown, where even the experts fall silent. If we gaze about us and see nothing but a tangle, we have not looked hard enough, we have not looked beyond our own deeds and needs to the order that sustains us. We may appeal to the headlines, or cite a disaster fallen on someone we love, and proclaim that the world makes no sense. Yet how could we be troubled by cancer, by hurricanes, by war, by all the messy ways in which things fall apart, if things did not cohere so amazingly to begin with? Of course we seek patterns, but the universe answers our seeking. What we call constellations are human shapes imposed on the stars, with names and legends attached; yet we did not invent the stars, nor their motions, nor their light. The question is not whether there is an order to the world, but what sort of order it is, whence it comes, how to speak of it, and how to live in relation to it.

Once when my father was studying a handful of dirt, I asked him if he had ever been lost. "No," he answered, "but there's been a few times when I didn't know where anything else was." By that definition, I am lost for days and weeks at a stretch, aware of myself but of little else. The only ground I notice is the grit under my shoes. The world is gray cardboard. I trudge through dullness, as though deep in a trench, wholly absorbed in taking the next step. Chores, chores, chores. Places to go, things to do.

Then occasionally I wake from my drowse and for a few minutes every toad becomes a dragon, every lilac is a fiery fountain, and I am walking on pure light.

These luminous moments are the standard by which I measure my ordinary hours. It may be the oldest human standard, older than the desire for comfort, older than duty. As the maverick monk Thomas Berry put it in his stiff but dignified way: "Awareness of an all-pervading mysterious energy articulated in the infinite variety of natural phenomena seems to be the primordial experience of human consciousness." *Energy* is a word that scientists willingly use, but *mystery* is not. Let mystery into the discussion, they fear, and pretty soon you'll have astral travel and bloodletting and witch hunts. You'll have fanatics reading the future in the bones of birds. You'll lock up Galileo for saying the earth spins about the sun. You'll hoot at Darwin for tracing our descent from the apes. You'll sweep away the magnificent, meticulous theater of science and replace it with a Punch-and-Judy show.

Cosmologists have tried every way they can to

avoid having to posit what they call "initial conditions"—those conditions that determine the features of our universe. Why, for example, does the proton have exactly this mass, why does the electron have that charge? Why does energy convert to matter and matter to energy? Why do the fundamental forces interact just so? Why does nature obey these rules, or any rules? Why are the parameters such that life could evolve, and, within life, consciousness? And how does it happen that consciousness has figured out so many of the rules?

If you admit that you cannot answer those questions and simply appeal to initial conditions in order to explain the founding features of the universe, then you raise the question of how those conditions were set. You bump into the old conundrum: How can there be a design without a designer? You can't do physics on God. So cosmologists have proposed a steady-state universe, an oscillating universe, or a universe with zero net energy sprung from quantum fluctuations, anything to avoid having to concede that reality extends beyond the reach of science.

With our twin hands, our paired eyes, our sense of a split between body and mind, we favor dualisms: design and designer, creation and creator, universe and God. But I suspect the doubleness is an illusion. "How can we know the dancer from the dance?" Yeats asked in "Among School Children." We hear treble and bass because we have two ears; the music itself is whole and undivided. The wind and the leaves shaking on the tree are two things; but the wave and the sea are one. When I sit on the pink granite of the Maine coast, stone and soul rubbed smooth by the stroke of water, I see the ocean ripple and surge into whitecaps. Just so, the earth is a wave lifted up from the surf of space, and you and I are waves lifted up from earth.

According to Hopi myth, long ago, at the beginning of our age, people emerged from a hole in the ground. They looked over the earth and liked what they saw, so they stayed. But at the end of time the people will go back again into the ground. When buried in graves or scattered as ashes, we also return to the ground. The throwing of the first shovelful of dirt on the coffin or the flinging of ash into the wind is a ritual moment when the earth reclaims us. Writing about the ground is in part an attempt to come to terms with death, with my own return to the source. But it is at least as much an attempt to come to terms with life, with the issuing-forth.

This is the light in which I have come to see Thoreau's best known sentence: "The West of which I speak is but another name for the Wild; and what I have been preparing to say is, that in Wildness is the preservation of the World." "Wildness" here is usually understood to mean wilderness. But I think it has a larger meaning. I think it refers to the creative energy that continually throws new forms into existence and gives them shape. Thus "Wildness" is literally the "preservation of the World," because without it there would *be* no world. Gary Snyder may have had some such notion in mind when he insisted in *The Practice of the Wild* that nature is simply what is, the way of things: "This, *thusness*, is the nature of the nature of nature. The wild in wild." By keeping in touch with wildness, we preserve our sanity and the world's health.

Beneath or behind or within everything there is an unfathomable ground—a suchness, as the Buddhists say—that one can point toward, bow to, contemplate, but cannot grasp. To speak of this ground as a mystery is not to say that we know nothing, only that we cannot know everything. The larger the context we envision, the more tentative and partial our knowledge appears, the more humble we are forced to be. Merely think of the earth as a living organism, taking the health of this great body as the gauge of everything we do, and you recognize that our ignorance is profound.

The thawing dirt brings me a whiff of the world's renewal. The green shoots of crocuses breaking through are the perennial thrusting-forth of shapeliness out of the void. Breathing in the breath of soil, I feel the force of Thomas Berry's claim that "Our deepest convictions arise in this contact of the human with some ultimate mystery whence the universe itself is derived." The smell brings to my lips the words my Mississippi grandfather used to say about anything that delighted him: "That suits me right down to the ground."

And yet, for all my conviction, I still get dizzy when I look down. Where oh where is that solid footing? On what rock can I build? Philosophers and theologians speak of the foundation of things as the ground of being. They go about like dowsers with divining rods, alert to every twitch in the forked stick. Here it is, one of them proclaims. No, it's over here, another insists. No, no, any fool can see it's right *here*. The quarrel among the dowsers is as old as speech, and most likely will continue as long as our breath holds out. What a seductive phrase: the ground of being. But if you waited to plant your beans or build your house until you had dug down to that elusive ground, you would go hungry and cold. I'll make do with the dirt I can touch.

The dirt I can touch beside my front door, where the grass needles through, is a mousy brown. If I lived elsewhere, the soil could be red, yellow, buff, or black. The colors of dirt are roughly the shades of human skin. I scoop a handful of it, gingerly, mindful of those billion organisms. Then I lift it to my face, sniff the damp, fruitful smell, and am glad.

CHAPTER SEVEN

TELLING
THE
HOLY

IN THAT PATCH OF OHIO between the military reservation and the Mahoning River, I lived as a boy in a neighborhood of unfinished houses, the neighbors having run out of money or gumption or time. Some houses rose no higher than the basement, a dank hole in which the family huddled like bears in a cave; others quit with a flimsy frame of two-by-fours, cloudy plastic over the windows, tar paper on the roof; still others, duly shingled and sided, waited years for chimneys or doorknobs or paint. There was a story of dismay or defeat behind every halted house: fathers laid off, mothers run off, children taken down by fever, a squall of babies, failed crops, bad bets, shootings and hauntings, whiskey, waste. Of all the stories, one I still find troubling concerns a man who quit work on his house because he had received what I have been listening for all my life, a clear message from God.

Let me call the man Jeremiah Lofts. Five days a week he worked in town at a factory that made balloons, Saturdays he did a little scrapedirt farming on his forty acres, and Sundays he preached in a concrete-block evangelical church. Even with three occupations, Lofts earned precious little. For years, he and his wife and their two, then four, and finally seven children lived in a rusting trailer on a bluff known as Ledge Hill. They had more dogs than children, more chickens than dogs, and the entire menagerie ran loose among a confusion of sheds, lumber piles, bald tires, and junked cars.

I knew the looks of their place because I hunted fossils in the creamy limestone of Ledge Hill, and I often stopped to drink from a spring that gushed into a trough where their dirt driveway met the road. It was a public spring, safe for drinking, according to a government sign posted there. Still a believer in government signs, I would lean over the mossy lip of the trough, sipping the icy water, and study the ramshackle homestead. In daydream and nightmare, afraid of sliding into poverty, I saw myself slinking through the pack of dogs, climbing the metal stairs, and opening the crooked door of their trailer.

Then one October Saturday when the corn was in the crib, Lofts borrowed a backhoe, dug trenches, and poured footings for a proper house. Week by week that fall and winter, with help from his congregation, he raised walls and roof, ran pipes and wires, and started laying brick. In January, the cold stopped the outside work, and then in February some force greater than cold stopped the inside work. Lofts laid down his tools, quit his job at the factory, bought no seed for planting, gave up every labor except preaching. He withdrew his children from school and locked his door against the truant officer. He forbade his wife and daughters and sons to speak with anyone outside the church. He left off shaving, and his beard grew in wiry and black.

We learned what force had stopped his work on the house, what shock had jolted him out of his old life, when Lofts turned up at our front door one frozen morning, dressed in his Sunday suit, to warn us all to repent, for the world would be coming to an end on the first day of July.

"End how?" my father asked.

"By holy fire," Lofts answered. "I was praying on Ledge Hill, and the Lord spoke to me from the stars."

"Did God say why?" my mother asked.

"Because we have been wicked in our use of the earth," Lofts replied, "and the Lord means to start over with new creatures."

He did not rant. He delivered the news firmly and simply, as a man might tell his neighbors about a coming storm. Father thanked him. Mother invited him in for coffee, but Lofts refused, explaining that he had a world of people still to warn.

I was nine or ten years old and easily spooked. I glanced from one parent to the other, trying to gauge how I should take this man's words. There was an iron conviction in his face and voice that kept my parents, and therefore me, from smiling. If God were to speak, why not to this scrapedirt farmer? Why not on Ledge Hill, where icy water poured unfailingly from the earth, where the fossils of sea creatures swam in stone? If, as newspapers and television and grown-ups declared, our long ingenious history had led only to H-bombs and race riots and war, why shouldn't the Creator begin afresh? If God were to announce a final fire, why not in the burning language of stars?

Between that February morning and the beginning of July, while Lofts delivered his warning door to door, I kept uneasy watch. Every rumor of tornadoes, every crack of lightning or grumble of thunder, every smudge of smoke on the horizon might be a token of the end.

While this great story of the world's fate played itself out, the small, everyday stories never ceased. The volunteer firemen held a pancake supper. A liquored-up father beat his kids, who limped into church all black and blue. Gas prices rose two cents a gallon. Lettuce bolted early from the heat. One of our ponies broke out of the pasture and swelled up from eating plums. The thirteen-year-old daughter of the woman who taught baton-twirling ran off with the son of the milkman. Attending to such ordinary stories in those apocalyptic days, however, was like trying to hear a drip against the roar of a waterfall.

On the eve of July first, Lofts withdrew into the shell of that half-built house to pray with his family. Whether he prayed for the world's salvation, or only for the salvation of his fellow believers, I cannot say. Whether any power heard him—whether any power capable of launching and extinguishing worlds *ever* hears a puny human voice—I do not know. I know only that the world survived, as the scoffers had insisted it would. Yet that survival seemed to me then, and seems to me now, at least as great a miracle as a dialogue with the Lord.

After the day of judgment passed without catastrophe, the prophet never showed his face in public again, not even at his church. The house was never finished. It stood for years, weeds sprouting among the unlaid bricks, tar paper curling loose from nails, paintless windows warping. Eventually the government bought the Lofts' forty acres, to be included in a park that would surround the new reservoir when the Mahoning River was dammed. One day the trailer was gone, along with the family, their chickens and dogs. A crew with a bulldozer and dump trucks flattened the shabby house, hauled away every last tire and timber and brick, and sowed grass in the raw dirt. The land soon reverted to meadow, the meadow to woods.

For the rest of my time in that neighborhood, I could not pass Ledge Hill, could not sip from the spring, could not chip fossils from the limestone road cut, without remembering the prophet. Even today, dozens of years and thousands of miles later, I remain attached to that place by the thread of his story. The smell of clay and moss, the ruckus of kids and crows and dogs, the rasp of rock against my fingers, the ache of icy water on my teeth, all these and countless other details remain with me, braided together by the prophet's story.

In the same way, other narrative threads, some

weak and some tough, connect me to every place I have known. Thus the Mahoning River, long-since dammed, still runs in me, because, one winter dawn while checking muskrat traps, I slipped into the chill current and nearly drowned. A field of wildflowers blooms in me because a woman who lived there alone in a cabin once filled my palm with seeds. In memory, a forest I have not seen for twenty years still murmurs with the voice of my father naming trees, a pasture gleams under the hooves of horses, a beach dimples under the footsteps of my wife. I am bound to the earth by a web of stories, just as I am bound to the creation by the very substance and rhythms of my flesh. By keeping the stories fresh, I keep the places themselves alive in my imagination. Living in me, borne in mind, these places make up the landscape on which I stand with familiarity and pleasure, the landscape over which I walk even when my feet are still.

I have been thinking about stories of place in an effort to understand how the geography of mind adheres to the geography of earth. Each of us carries an inward map on which are inscribed, as on Renaissance charts, the seas and continents known to us. On my own map, the regions where I have lived most attentively are crowded with detail, while regions I have only glimpsed from windows or imagined from hearsay are barely sketched, and out at the frontiers of my knowledge the lines dwindle away into blankness.

There are certain spots on my map where many lines converge, like roads leading to a capitol, or like rays of energy streaming from a center of power.

Ledge Hill is one such spot. I have recalled the story of the prophet because both the man and his place carry for me a tingle of the sacred. I do not claim that Jeremiah Lofts actually heard from God, only that he was listening for the profoundest speech. His business was with the ultimate ground. So is mine, however clumsy I may be.

Traditional peoples distinguish between tales of the everyday world and tales of the spirit world, between history and myth, between profane and sacred. The distinction rests, of course, on a belief that there *is* a spirit world, an order that infuses and informs the changing surfaces we see. Visions of that sustaining realm may be sought through spiritual discipline, but they may not be summoned. If they come, they come as gifts, unforeseen. By telling stories, we conserve the memory of their passing, and we prepare ourselves for the next illumination.

I am aware of some grave objections to stories in general and to sacred stories in particular. In *Aspects of the Novel*, E. M. Forster offers an opinion that is common among literary sophisticates when he refers to story as "this low atavistic form." According to Forster, stories preserve "the voice of the tribal narrator, squatting in the middle of the cave, and saying one thing after another until the audience falls asleep among their offal and bones. The story is primitive, it reaches back to the origins of literature, before reading was discovered, and it appeals to what is primitive in us." Over the past century, our craving for story has provoked sighs from the likes of Henry James, Gustav Flaubert, James Joyce, Vladimir Nabokov, and Samuel Beckett. Their sighing proclaims them to be civilized, modern, free from illusion; they have left the cave to dwell outside, where stories shrivel in the harsh light of reason.

As for a belief in the sacred, that, too, according to many scholars, is a holdover from our benighted past. In *Cosmos and History*, Mircea Eliade argues that myth, ritual, taboo, every grasping for a transcendent reality, merely expresses our desire to abolish time, to resist change, to escape mortality. Nowhere is the desire to escape from the "terror of history" more nakedly revealed, Eliade claims, than in "primitive" societies. His examination of the uses of myth in ancient cultures leads him to a rhetorical question: "May we conclude from all this that, during this period, humanity was still within nature; had not yet detached itself from nature?" The moral is clear: so long as we seek an order outside of time, we remain primitive, childish, perilously close to the beasts; only by detaching ourselves from nature, weaning ourselves from sacred stories, and accepting the terror of history as the sole reality, can we become fully human.

Having read Eliade, not to mention Freud and Jung, one would be hard pressed to deny the psychological component of myth. But to go to the opposite extreme, and claim that myth is *nothing but* a projection of psychic dramas, is equally simplistic, and perhaps more dangerous. The danger is that in our narcissism we will be content to speak and think and care only about ourselves. Joseph Campbell avoids both extremes by arguing that myth enacts two dramas at once, that of our psyche and that of nature. In *The*

Hero with a Thousand Faces, Campbell surveys the sacred stories from many ages and cultures to suggest that mythology speaks not only about the unconscious but also about the cosmos:

> Briefly formulated, the universal doctrine teaches that all the visible structures of the world—all things and beings—are the effects of a ubiquitous power out of which they rise, which supports and fills them during the period of their manifestation, and back into which they must ultimately dissolve. This is the power known to science as energy, to the Melanesians as *mana,* to the Sioux Indians as *wakonda,* the Hindus as *shakti,* and the Christians as the power of God. Its manifestation in the psyche is termed, by the psychoanalysts, *libido.* And its manifestation in the cosmos is the structure and flux of the universe itself.

This is the belief that Barry Lopez found among hunting peoples, that Bruce Chatwin found among the Aborigines of Australia. You can hear it voiced by the Kiowa novelist, N. Scott Momaday; by the Zen master, Thich Nhat Hanh; or by the Christian mystic, Thomas Merton. You can find it in the essays of the biologist, René Dubos, of the anthropologist, Loren Eiseley, and of the physicist, Freeman Dyson. You can trace it everywhere in Emerson's work, as when in "The American Scholar" he asks, "What is nature?" and answers, "There is never a beginning, there is never an end, to the inexplicable continuity of this web of God, but always circular power returning into itself." In their various accents, these voices declare that a spiritual landscape does indeed flicker and flame within the physical one.

I believe that this doctrine is widespread because it is true, or at least it is as close to the truth as we have been able to come. Sacred stories arise from our intuition that beneath the flow of creation there is order, within change there is permanence, within time there is eternity. Everything moves; yet everything is shapely. The Apache word for myth means literally "to tell the holiness." By telling the holy, sacred stories ground a people or an individual, not merely in a landscape, but in the power that creates and preserves the land.

If *all* of creation is holy, if one power flows everywhere—through psyche and cyclotron, through grass and granite—then why do we identify certain groves, mountains, or springs as sacred? Because they concentrate our experience of the land. We cannot hold the entire earth or even a forest or river in our minds at once; we need smaller places to apprehend and visit. We go to such places in thought or flesh to dream, to renew our strength, to remind ourselves of the source of all things; we go there as Jeremiah Lofts went to the stony crown of Ledge Hill, to seek the power that made us.

Pilgrims often journey to the ends of the earth in search of holy ground, only to find that they have never walked on anything else. Here, for an eloquent example, is what Peter Matthiessen discovered in Tibet, where he went in search of the snow leopard and enlightenment:

The search may begin with a restless feeling, as if one were being watched. One turns in all directions and sees nothing. Yet one senses that there is a source for this deep restlessness; and the path that leads there is not a path to a strange place, but the path home. . . . The journey is hard, for the secret place *where we have always been* is overgrown with thorns and thickets of "ideas," of fears and defenses, prejudices and repressions.

I have spied that secret place from time to time, usually as through a glass darkly, but now and again with blazing clarity. One time it glowed from a red carnation, incandescent in a florist's window. Once it shimmered in drifting pollen, once in a sky needled with ice. I have seen it wound in a scarf of dust around a whirling pony. I have seen it glinting from a pebble on the slate bed of a creek. I have slipped into that secret place while watching hawks, while staring down the throat of a lily, while brushing my wife's hair. Metaphors are inexact. The experience is not a glimpsing of realms beyond, nor of becoming someone new, but of acknowledging, briefly and utterly, who I am.

Barry Lopez, another pilgrim, has traveled from the Arctic to the Antarctic in his own search for an understanding of how to live wisely within the natural order. In all his travels, he has found that wisdom embodied in stories:

The aspiration of aboriginal people throughout the world has been to achieve a congruent relationship with the land, to fit well in it. To achieve occasionally a state of high harmony or reverberation. The dream of this transcendent congruency included the evolution of a hunting and gathering relationship with the earth, in which a mutual regard was understood to prevail; but it also meant a conservation of the stories that bind the people into the land.

Against those who warn us, as Forster and Eliade do, that a respect for myth and a hankering for the sacred are throwbacks to our dim origins, I appeal to the testimony of such witnesses as Lopez and Matthiessen, and to my own grounding experiences. If to be modern is to give up inquiring about my true home, then let me remain archaic. The root of *primitive*, as Gary Snyder points out, is *primus*, "or 'first,' like 'original mind,' original human society, original way of being." Sacred places, and the stories we tell about them, put us back in touch with what is original, in ourselves and in creation.

For all my conviction, the watchdog of reason inside me still raises its hackles whenever I talk about stories, and when I talk about the sacred it bares its fangs and barks. Where are the hard data? it snarls—for this is a talking watchdog, straight out of fairy tale—where's the proof? Where are the equations? the formulas? Where, oh where, are the *numbers*?

Anyone who tries to live by stories—by hearing, by reading, and especially by making them—is likely to be nagged by the yapping of doubt. Hasn't science made myth obsolete? Even someone as firm in her vocation as Flannery O'Connor admitted feeling "a certain embarrassment about being a storyteller in these times when stories are considered not quite as satisfying as statements and statements not quite as satisfying as statistics."

I very much doubt that we can live by statements, and I am certain we cannot live by statistics. Not even scientists can bear a steady diet of numbers. After Ruth comes home from the lab, we often talk over the day's experiments as we are fixing dinner, and she will often say, when the results have been confusing, that she and her colleagues haven't yet figured out a plausible story for the data. The data themselves only make sense, only add up to knowledge, when they are embodied in narrative. An equation is a miniature plot: this causes that, which causes that, which causes that.

The larger the field of explanation, the more obvious the role of narrative. Darwin's *Origin of Species* is a story about life on earth, and Edward O. Wilson's *Sociobiology* is a story about human nature, and Stephen Hawking's *Brief History of Time* is a story of the universe. Reading one account after another, we try to make a picture of the whole by stitching the tales together. In claiming that science is a patchwork of stories, I am not saying it is untrue; on the contrary, I am saying that scientists, like the rest of us, have no way of snaring truth, no way of carrying it around, no way of storing it, except in stories.

The resemblance between science and myth is most obvious at the boundaries of knowledge, where science pushes at the limits of what can be tested by our present equipment. Many current theories about the smallest constituents of matter, about the very early universe, about the nature of energy and time, appear to be untestable not merely by our present equipment but by any equipment we could conceivably build. For a physicist such as James Gunn, this is cause for lament:

> The big problem, it seems to me, is that there is such a plethora of possible theoretical frameworks at the moment and no way of testing them. The subject is sort of running open loop. That's not very healthy from a purely scientific point of view. It's very exciting, but from the point of view of trying to learn the "truth," I think we've taken a large step backward.

Poets and painters, novelists and musicians know only too well how it feels to choose among a plethora of frameworks. To add a single stroke, a note, a word can be an agony of decision. No gauge will tell us which of our inventions work and which ones fail. The artist swims—or drowns—in possibilities.

"The maker of a sentence," as Emerson put it grandly, "launches out into the infinite and builds a road into Chaos and old Night, and is followed by those who hear him with something of wild, creative delight." I think of my own sentences not as roads, not even as dirt tracks with a fringe of grass up the middle, but as faint, meandering paths. Comparing the scratches I have made to the infinite that surrounds me, I am reminded of Chuang Tzu's warning:

> *You are trying to sound*
> *The middle of the ocean*
> *With a six-foot pole.*

No pole will reach the bottom. No number of sentences or brush strokes or musical notes will ever exhaust old Night. Art is so tentative, so quirky, so measly compared to the universe, that only a fool would mistake it for the truth.

Many scientists, however, seem to grasp for a truth unencumbered by doubt, by mystery, a truth as plain as the hand in front of your face. "One can take various philosophical attitudes towards the nature of the truth," the astronomer Edwin Turner said in a recent interview,

> but if we take the most simplistic view of an external reality that has some truth value, and consider that our job as scientists is to try to get hold of that, I think that a hard-nosed rationalist might conclude that the job is too hard for us. There is much interesting and true stuff about the universe that we will never learn, or not in a foreseeable time. As I said, much of what we currently believe may well be wrong, or at least we won't be able to find out whether it's true or not.

This will seem a large step backward only if you imagine that science has *ever* given us an unambiguous, unadorned, exhaustive picture of things. If you believe, as I do, that science, like art, has always been a tissue of stories—intricate, dazzling, and incomplete—then for us to admit the limitations of our knowledge may be a step forward.

So I carve the word *mystery* on a bone and throw it to the watchdog of reason. The dog stares at me, sniffs the bone, then sullenly chews, lips curled, ready at any moment to rear on its haunches and bark.

Mystery is not much in favor these days. The notion that there are limits to what we can do, what we can know, limits to our dominion, does not sit well with kings and queens of the hill. Humility and reverence, we hear, are the attitudes of cowards. Why worship a force we cannot measure on a meter? Why tell stories about a power we cannot photograph? Flannery O'Connor once revealed to a correspondent that her "gravest concern" was "the conflict between an attraction for the Holy and the disbelief in it that we breathe in with the air of the times." I feel that attraction for the holy, and my throat, too, burns with the air of disbelief.

When the novelist Reynolds Price published his translations of stories from the Bible in a book called *A Palpable God*, he prefaced it with a long meditation on "The Origins and Life of Narrative," in which he sought to explain why a cultivated person in our secular age might still take seriously these old tales of the holy. The "first—and final—aim of narrative," he argued, is "compulsion of belief in an ordered world." Of course it would be reassuring to believe in an ordered world, say the skeptics. But what if the universe is chaotic, a hazard of bits and pieces, and our tales of order are but soothing lullabies we sing against the darkness?

That line of reasoning leads to what I think of as the killjoy critique of sacred stories: they must be false because they are comforting. They are not, in fact, all comforting. Many are frightening. In myths, gods appear and disappear, play tricks, throw tantrums, devour the innocent and reward the wicked, bewilder the most patient seeker. The holy is often a holy terror. Still, the killjoy critique is forceful, as Reynolds Price acknowledged: "Human narrative, through all its visible length, gives emphatic signs of arising from the profoundest need of one fragile species. Sacred story is the perfect answer given by the world to the hunger of that species for true consolation." Mustn't so perfect an answer be an illusion? Not necessarily, Price added, for "the fact that we hunger has not precluded food." Water is nonetheless real for slaking our thirst, lovemaking nonetheless real for meeting our desire. I do not doubt the sun, even though it warms me and lights my way. Yes, tales about a holy power may satisfy our craving for consolation, but that proves nothing about the truth of the tales or the reality of the power.

The order we glimpse through myths is one that we did not create, that we cannot alter, that we can never fully grasp, and that we ignore at our peril. The achievements of science delude many into thinking that we have graduated from nature, that we can understand everything, that we can change or scorn conditions as we see fit, that we are the bosses of the universe. Among those who resist this delusion of omnipotence are a number of scientists. The physicist Charles Misner, for example, has articulated a humbler view:

> I do see the design of the universe as essentially a religious question. That is, one should have some kind of respect and awe for the whole business, it seems to me. It's very magnificent and shouldn't be taken for granted. In fact, I believe that is why Einstein had so little use for organized religion, although he strikes me as a basically very religious man. He must have looked at what the preachers said about God and felt that they were blaspheming. He had seen much more majesty than they had ever imagined.

By "mystery" I do not mean simply the blank places on our maps. I mean the divine source—not a void, not a darkness, but an uncapturable fullness. We are sustained by processes and powers that we can neither fathom nor do without. I speak of that ground as holy because it is ultimate, it is what makes us possible, what shapes and upholds everything we see. The stories I am most interested in hearing, reading, and telling, are those that help us imagine our lives in relation to that ground.

By telling the holy, we acknowledge that life is a gift. In fact, the whole universe is a gift. From where or what, and why, we cannot know. All we *do* know is that it issues forth, moment by moment, eon by eon, ever fresh, astounding in its richness and beauty. None of this is to gainsay the pain, the suffering, the eventual death that awaits all created things. But we measure that pain and suffering, we mourn that death, against the sheer exuberant flow of things. We can lose our life only because it has been given to us.

"The plants, rocks, fire, water, all are alive," says an Apache storyteller. "They watch us and see our needs. They see when we have nothing to protect us, and it is then that they reveal themselves and speak to us."

Oh, that things would reveal themselves and speak to us! Such was the yearning, I feel certain, that led Jeremiah Lofts to kneel on top of Ledge Hill and led me to remember his story and his place all these years. Such is the yearning that leads me outdoors to embrace the backyard maple, or to dance in the rain, or to taste the dirt. Judging by folklore and myth, this is a perennial human desire, to converse with our neighbors in their separate dialects—to speak bear with bear, oak with oak, flint with flint—and once in a great while to leap into the universal language and hear and be heard by the Creator.

In the beginning, storytellers say, humans and animals could speak to one another, as familiarly as God spoke with Adam and Eve in the garden. The lore of many lands is filled with helpful coyotes or cats, talkative serpents or swans, wise lions, crafty crows. Even the villains—the dragons and wolves—are garrulous. Now and again a wild poet such as Blake may still converse with tigers, or a shaman such as Black Elk may still converse with buffaloes. But the rest of us have forgotten the universal language. Our ears have been stopped up. Our lips are sealed.

Nature is noisy, all right, and it moves in patterns,

but neither sounds nor movements seem to be addressed to us. The racket the world makes is either pure babble—as in the crash of waves, the crackle of lightning, the sizzle of wind through trees, the static from stars—or else it is a language not meant for human ears, as in the calls of dolphins and owls. There are no messages for us in the dance of quarks, no morals in the genetic code, no sermons in the sunset. Like refugees washed up on a foreign shore, we spy and eavesdrop on nature, searching for clues, trying to decipher an alien tongue. According to Hindus, God speaks Sanskrit; according to Jews, God speaks Hebrew; according to one people after another, God speaks the language of the tribe. What God speaks, I humbly submit, is the universe. Since nobody has supplied us with a cosmic dictionary, we have been laboring, word by word, over a thousand generations, to compile one for ourselves.

As I sit here this morning, sounding the ocean with my six-foot pole, my daughter sits on the grass in an aviary a few miles away, observing starlings. Eva translates their clatter, their prancing and preening, into a code that her research team can understand. When the starlings wake before their caretakers arrive, she says, the birds will imitate the noise of doors opening, feet scuffling, grain being poured. That is a code even I can understand. Make the right sounds and, sure enough, the humans show up with breakfast. Our own dances and songs may be just as transparent to a mind more comprehensive than ours.

Stories about a time when we spoke easily with starlings and sycamores, with mountains and mountain goats, with our Creator in the garden, arise, I suspect, not from a memory of what was, but from a longing for what might be. Oh, that things would reveal themselves and speak to us! Why else do we teach sign language to chimpanzees? Why else do we lower microphones into the ocean to record the arias of whales? Why do we break atoms to bits and scrutinize the pieces? Why send probes into space? Why stare, through telescopes, at the wink of pulsars?

According to a theory favored by many physicists, the universe bloomed from the breaking of symmetries in the first smidgen of a second after the Big Bang. Symmetry breaking led to the preponderance of matter over anti-matter, the clumping of stuff into stars and galaxies, and the division of a single force into the four we observe (gravity, electromagnetism, strong and weak nuclear forces). Myths likewise tell us that originally there was a unity, and now there is a scatter; originally there was no break between life and ground, between creatures and Creator, and now there is estrangement. When Buddhism speaks about recognizing our true Self, or Taoism about centering ourselves in the Way, or Judaism about Eden before the Fall, or Christianity about being One in Christ, they point, longingly, toward an unbroken symmetry, a primal unity.

Thomas Merton remarked on that longing in a letter to a Buddhist friend: "In any event, there is only one meeting place for all religions, and it is paradise. How nice to be there and wander about looking at the flowers. Or being the flowers." Paradise is not a place but a condition, a simple being-alive, a drinking straight from the spring. Animals seem to fill their skins, trees their bark, rivers their banks, so beautifully, that we cannot help but see in their wildness a perfect at-homeness. The words *holy* and *healthy* have the same root, which means *whole*. We perceive in nature an integrity which is our birthright, a unity in which we already participate, in which we cannot help but participate.

After admitting her embarrassment about being a storyteller in an age that preferred statements and statistics, Flannery O'Connor added that "in the long run, a people is known, not by its statements or its statistics, but by the stories it tells." By what stories shall we be known?

Within a mile or two of Ledge Hill, along the banks of the Mahoning River, I used to help a farmer named Sivvy collect buckets of sap from his grove of maples. We emptied the buckets into a barrel that rode on a sledge pulled by twin draft horses. Mr. Sivvy preferred using horses, he explained to me, because the noise of a tractor would have disturbed the trees. It would certainly have disturbed Mr. Sivvy, who spoke to the team of dappled gray Percherons with clicks of his tongue and soft words. As we worked, he told me tales about the horses, about the maples, about the river that muscled through his farm, about the clouds, the frogs, the thawing dirt. Here is what the soil needs, he told me, here is what the rains do, here is what dogwood and larkspur say about the condition of the woods. All his actions, from plowing to pruning, were informed and constrained by what he knew of his place.

Until the government built a dam and flooded Mr. Sivvy's farm, every year the maples yielded their sap without diminution, every year the soil was richer, the pastures were thicker, the birds more abundant. He lived well on his piece of earth because he was married to it by narrative as well as by nature. So might we marry ourselves to a place, commune with other creatures, make ourselves at home through stories.

We live in a land that has been known, remembered, spoken of with reverence and joy for thousands of years. Only in the last few generations has the land disappeared from our speech. In my own region of the Ohio Valley, there are few traces left of the aboriginal way. As the Shawnee, Miami, and other tribes were driven out, by arms or treaty, we lost the benefit of their long-evolved knowledge of the animals, the plants, the seasons, the soil itself. We lost nearly all of their stories and songs.

I am reminded of that loss when I read about efforts to reestablish bighorn sheep in the mountain and desert regions of the American West. Time and again, a goodly sized herd has been released into an area where bighorns once flourished, but then, year by year, their numbers dwindle away. The problem, it turns out, is that the sheep do not know how to move between their summer range and their winter range, and so they starve. Biologists can put the sheep in ideal habitat, can rig them with radio collars, can inoculate them against disease, but cannot teach them the migration routes, which bighorns learn only from other bighorns. Once the link between sheep and ground is broken, and the memory of the trails is lost, there seems to be no way of restoring it.

We can lie to ourselves about many things; but if we lie about our relationship to the land, the land will suffer, and soon we and all other creatures that share the land will suffer. If we persist in our ignorance or dishonesty, we will die, as surely as those bighorns perish from not knowing where they are. We are smarter than sheep, in most respects. Seeing the danger of ignorance, we may be moved to invent or recover some of the lore that connects us to the land, that tells us how to live in our place.

Right now, here and there throughout America, tough-minded people are trying to reconstruct a survival lore for their own territory, their own watersheds, their own neighborhoods. I think of Robert Finch and John Hay on Cape Cod, of John Hanson Mitchell in Massachusetts, Edward Hoagland in Vermont, Wendell Berry in Kentucky, Wes Jackson in Kansas. I think of Terry Tempest Williams in Utah, Gary Nabhan in Arizona, Leslie Silko in New Mexico, Gary Snyder in California, Gretel Ehrlich in Wyoming, Ursula Le Guin in Oregon, Robert Michael Pyle in Washington, Richard Nelson and John Haines in Alaska. I think of more people than I have space to name. Whatever their training, they are all cartographers of sorts, drawing maps of particular places, giving us narratives that reveal the lay of the land, that show how the power moves, that guide us to sustenance and beauty.

In telling the holy, we do not *acquire* power, as one might gather coins in one's purse, but we acknowledge it, join with it, dwell *in* the power. The Aborigines of Australia believe that they help renew the world by recalling stories and singing songs from the beginning time. Their dreaming tracks are paths they walk and tales they tell, paths of footsteps and narrative drawn on the land. They participate in the ongoing work of nature by reaffirming the creation. "In Aboriginal belief," Bruce Chatwin reports, "an unsung land is a dead land: since, if the songs are forgotten, the land itself will die. To allow that to happen was the worst of all possible crimes."

As we walk our own ground, on foot or in mind, we need to be able to recite stories about hills and trees and animals, stories that root us in this place and that keep it alive. The sounds we make, the patterns we draw, the plots we trace may be as native to the land as deer trails or bird songs. The more fully we belong to our place, the more likely that our place will survive without damage. We cannot create myth from scratch, but we can recover or fashion stories that will help us to see where we are, how others have lived here, how we ourselves should live.

CHAPTER EIGHT

WAYLAND

NOT FAR FROM LEDGE Hill where Jeremiah Lofts spoke with God, a few miles downriver from Sivvy's farm where the draft horses hauled barrels filled with maple sap, two blacktop roads, broken by frost and mended with tar, running from nowhere to nowhere, cross at right angles in the rumpled farm country of northeastern Ohio. The neighborhood where they intersect is called Wayland—not a village, not even a hamlet, only a cluster of barns and silos and frame houses and a white steepled Methodist church. Just north of Wayland, the Army fenced in fifty square miles of ground for their bomb factory, and just to the south the Corps of Engineers built their reservoir. I grew up behind those government fences in the shadows of bunkers, and on

farms that have since vanished beneath those government waters. Family visits to church began carrying
me to Wayland when I was five, romance was carrying
me there still at seventeen, and in the years between I
was drawn there often by duty or desire. Thus it happened that within shouting distance of the Wayland
crossroads I met seven of the great mysteries.

Even as a boy, oblivious much of the time to all save
my own sensations, I knew by the tingle in my spine
when I had bumped into something utterly new. I
groped for words to describe what I had felt, as I grope
still. Since we give labels to all that puzzles us, as we
name every blank space on the map, I could say that
what I stumbled into in Wayland were the mysteries of
death, life, beasts, food, mind, sex, and God. But
these seven words are only tokens, worn coins that I
shove onto the page, hoping to bribe you, coins I finger as reminders of those awful encounters.

The roads that cross at Wayland are too humble to
show on the Ohio map, too small even to wear numbers. And yet, without maps or mistakes, without
quite meaning to, I recently found my way back there
from several hundred miles away, after an absence of
twenty-five years, led along the grooves of memory.

The grooves are deep, and they set me vibrating
well before I reached the place, as the spiral cuts in
phonograph records will shake music from a needle. I
was heading toward Cleveland when I took a notion to
veer off the interstate and see what had become of Akron, which led me to see what had become of Kent,
which led me to Ravenna, the seat of Portage County.
Nothing aside from stoplights made me pause. Not

sure what I was looking for, I drove east from the county seat along a highway hurtling with trucks. Soon the rusted chain-link fence of the Ravenna Arsenal came whipping by on my left, and the raised bed of the Baltimore & Ohio tracks surged by on the right. Then I realized where I was going. My knuckles whitened on the steering wheel as I turned from the highway, put my back toward the trucks and bombs, and passed under the railroad through a concrete arch. Beyond the arch, the woods and fields and houses of Wayland shimmered in the October sunlight, appearing to my jealous eye scarcely changed after a quarter of a century.

I knew the place had changed, of course, if only because in the years since I had come here last—drawn in those days like a moth to the flame of a girl—the population of the earth had nearly doubled. Every crossroads, every woods, every field on the planet is warping under the pressure of our terrible hunger. So I knew that Wayland had changed, for all its pastoral shimmer in the autumn light. Yet I was grateful that on the surface it so much resembled my childhood memories, for, in my effort to live adequately in the present, I had come here to conduct some business with the past. What had brought me back to Wayland was a need to dig through the fluff and debris of ordinary life, down to some bedrock of feeling and belief.

I left my car in the graveled parking lot of the church and set out walking. Without planning my steps, I meandered where memory led, and where it led was from station to station of my childhood astonishment.

Not yet ready for the church, I went next door to the parsonage, where I had first caught a whiff of death. The two-story house—covered in white asbestos siding and plain as a box of salt, with a porch across the front and a green gabled roof—could have belonged to any of the neighboring farms. That was appropriate, for the ministers who succeeded one another in the house often preached as though they were farmers, weeding out sins, harvesting souls.

The minister whom I knew first was the Reverend Mr. Knipe, a bulky man sunken with age, his hair as white as the siding on the parsonage, his voice like the cooing of pigeons in the barn. Much in life amused him. Whenever he told you something that struck him as funny, he would cover his mouth with a hand to hide his smile. Despite the raised hand, often his laugh burst free and rolled over you. I began listening to him preach and pray and lead hymns when I was five, and for the next two years I heard Reverend Knipe every Sunday, until his voice became for me that of the Bible itself, even the voice of God. Then one Sunday when I was seven, I shook his great hand after the service as usual, suffering him to bend down and pat my head, and I went home to my dinner and he went home to his. While his wife set the table in the parsonage, Reverend Knipe rested on the front porch in his caned rocking chair, drifted off to sleep, and never woke up.

When Mother told me of this, the skin prickled on my neck. To sleep and never wake! To be a white-haired man with a voice like a barnful of pigeons, and the next minute to be nothing at all! Since my parents considered me too young to attend the funeral, I could only imagine what had become of his body, and I imagined not decay but evaporation—the flesh dispersing into thin air like morning mist from a pond.

The following Sunday, while a visitor preached, I stole away from church and crept over to the parsonage. I drew to the edge of the porch, rested my chin on the railing, and stared at the empty rocker. Reverend Knipe will never sit in that chair again, I told myself. Never, never, never. I tried to imagine how long forever would last. I tried to imagine how it would feel to be nothing. No thing. Suddenly chair and house and daylight vanished, and I was gazing into a dark hole, I was falling, I was gone. I caught a whiff of death, the damp earthy smell seeping from beneath the porch. It was also the smell of mud, of leaping grass, of spring. Clinging to that sensation, I pulled myself up out of the hole. There was the house again, the chair. I lifted my chin from the railing, swung away, and ran back to the church, chanting to myself: He was old and I am young, he was old and I am young.

Nights, often, and sometimes in the broad light of day, I still have to scrabble up out of that hole. We all do. In childhood, early or late, each of us bangs head-on into the blank fact we call death. Once that collision takes place, the shock of it never wears off. We may find ourselves returning to the spot where it occurred as to the scene of an accident, the way I found myself drawn, half a lifetime later, to the front steps of this parsonage. I was a stranger to the family who lived there now. Not wishing to intrude on them, I paused by the steps and surveyed the porch. An aluminum folding chair had replaced the rocker. I squatted by the railing, lowering my face to the height of a seven-year-old, closed my eyes against the shadows, and sniffed. From below the sill of the porch came the earth's dank perennial breath, fetid and fertile. Yes, I thought, filling myself with the smell: this abides, this is real; no matter the name we give it, life or death, it is a fact as rough and solid as a stone squeezed in the palm of the hand.

A dog yapped inside the parsonage. I stood up hurriedly and backed away, before anyone could appear at the door to ask me what in tarnation I was looking for under that porch.

Still following the grooves of memory, I crossed the road to stand in the driveway of another house, this one a motley bungalow encased in stone and aluminum. It was not so much the house that drew me as it was the side yard, where, about this time each fall, we brought our apples for pressing. The old press with its wooden vat and iron gears used to balance on concrete blocks in the shade of a weeping willow. We would pick apples in the Arsenal, from orchards that had been allowed to go wild after the government bulldozed the farmsteads. Unsprayed, blotched and wormy, these apples were also wonderfully sweet. We kept them in bushel baskets and cardboard boxes in the cellar, their fragrance filling the house, until we had accumulated enough to load our station wagon. Then we drove here, parked beside the willow, and fed our fruit into the press.

On this mild October day, the willow looked as I remembered it, thick in the trunk and gold in the leaves.

There was no sign of a press, but that did not keep me from remembering what it was like to squeeze apples. First we pulped them in a mill, then we wrapped them in cheesecloth and tamped them down, layer by layer, into the slotted wooden vat. To mash them, we spun a cast-iron wheel. It was easy to begin with, so easy that my brother and sister and I could make the spokes whirl. Later, the cranking would become too hard for us, and our mother would take her turn, then our father, then both of them together. The moment that set me trembling, however, came early on, while my hand was still on the iron wheel, the moment when cider began to ooze through the cheesecloth, between the slats, and down the spout into a waiting bucket. Out of the dirt, out of the gnarled trunks and wide-flung branches, out of the ripe red fruit had come this tawny juice. When my arms grew tired, I held a Mason jar under the spout, caught a glassful, and drank it down. It was as though we had squeezed the planet and out had poured sweetness.

What came back to me, musing there by the willow all these years later, was the sound of cider trickling into the bucket, the honeyed taste of it, and my bewilderment that rain and wood and dirt and sun had yielded this juice. Amazing, that we can drink the earth! Amazing, that it quenches our thirst, answers our hunger! Who would have predicted such an outlandish thing? Who, having sipped, can forget that it is the earth we swallow?

Well, I had forgotten; or at least I had buried under the habits of casual eating that primal awareness of the meaning of food. And so here was another fundamental perception, renewed for me by my sojourn in Wayland. This image of cider gushing from a spout was my cornucopia, proof of the dazzling abundance that sustains us.

From the cider house I walked downhill to the crossroads. One corner was still a pasture, browsed by three horses, another was a scrubby field grown up in brush and weeds, and the other two corners were expansive lawns. Through the brushy field meandered a creek where I used to hunt frogs with a flashlight and bucket. As in all the Octobers I could remember, the maples in the yards were scarlet, the pasture oaks were butterscotch, and the sycamores along the creek were stripped down to their voluptuous white limbs. Yellow mums and bright red pokers of salvia were still thriving in flowerbeds. A portly older man on a riding mower was cutting one of the lawns, while from a stump beside the driveway an older woman observed his progress, a hand shading her eyes. I knew them from childhood, but their names would not come. I waved, and they waved back. That was conversation enough. I had no wish to speak with them or with anyone in Wayland, since I would have been hard put to explain who I was or why I had come back. Maybe I also wanted to keep the past pure, unmixed with the present.

Because the crossroads are laid out on the grid of survey lines, the blacktop runs due north and south, east and west. The roads were so little traveled that I could stand in the intersection, the tar gummy beneath my boots, and gaze along the pavement in each of the cardinal directions. I had just come from the south, where the church gleamed on its hill. My view to the north was cut off by the railroad, except for the arched opening of the underpass, through which I could see the rusted fence of the Arsenal. Memories of a girl I had courted were beckoning from the west; but less feverish memories beckoned from the opposite direction, and that is where I chose to go next.

A quarter mile east of the crossroads I came to a farm where the Richards family used to breed and board and train horses. Although the name on the mailbox had changed, ten or twelve horses were grazing, as before, in a paddock beside the barn. I leaned against the slat fence and admired them.

In boyhood I had raised and ridden horses of my own, a stocky mixture of Shetland pony and the high-stepping carriage breed known as hackney. They all came out of a single ornery mare called Belle, and they all had her color, a sorrel coat that grew sleek in summer and shaggy in winter. We used to bring Belle here to the Richards' place for mating with a hackney stallion. Years before the voltage of sex began to make my own limbs jerk, I had been amazed by the stallion's fervor and the mare's skittishness. He nipped and nuzzled and pursued her; she danced and wheeled. Their energy seemed too great for the paddock to hold. Surely the fence would give way, the barn itself would fall! Then at length Belle shivered to a standstill and allowed the stallion to lift his forelegs onto her rump, his back legs jigging, hoofs scrabbling for purchase, her legs opening to his dark pizzle, the two of them momentarily one great plunging beast. And then, if luck held, eleven or twelve months later Belle would open her legs once more and drop a foal. Within minutes of entering the world, the foal would be tottering about on its wobbly stilts, drunk on air, and it would be ramming its muzzle into Belle's belly in search of milk. What a world, that the shivering union of mare and stallion in the barnyard should lead to this new urgency!

Musing there by the paddock on this October afternoon, I felt toward the grazing horses a huge affection. Each filled its hide so gloriously. I gave a low whistle. Several massive heads bobbed up and swung toward me, jaws working on grass, ears pricked forward. Their black eyes regarded me soberly, then all but one of the heads returned to grazing. The exception was a palomino gelding, who tossed his white mane, switched his white tail, and started ambling in my direction. As he drew near, I stretched my right arm toward him, palm open. Had I known I would be coming here, I would have brought apples or sugar cubes. My father would have pulled a cigarette from his pocket and offered that. But all I had to offer was the salt on my skin. The palomino lowered his muzzle to my palm, sniffed cautiously, then curled out his rasping red tongue and licked.

I knew that sandpapery stroke on my hand as I knew few other sensations. Just so, my own horses had nibbled up oats and sugar and sweat from my palm. The pressure of their tongues made my whole body sway. There by the fence, past and present merged, and I was boy and man, swaying. I reveled in the muscular touch, animal to animal. Contact! It assured me that I was not alone in the world. I was a creature among creatures.

When the palomino lost interest in my right hand, I offered my left. He sniffed idly, and, finding it empty, turned back to the greater temptation of grass. But the rasp of his tongue on my palm stayed with me, another clean, hard fact, another piece of bedrock on which to build a life.

The field across the road from the Richards place was grown up into a young woods, mostly staghorn sumac and cedar and oak. When I had seen it last, twenty-five years earlier, this had been a meadow luxuriant with grasses and wildflowers. Back where the far edge of the field ran up against the sinuous line of willows bordering the creek, there had been a cottage, low and brown, moss growing on the roof, weeds lapping at the windows, a place that looked from a distance more like a forgotten woodpile than a house. Today, no cottage showed above the vigorous trees. But near my feet I could see the twin ruts of the dirt track that led back to the place. I followed them, my boots knocking seeds from thistle and wild rye.

I knew the meadow and the cottage because the woman who used to live here was my science teacher in high school. Fay Givens must have been in her early sixties when I met her in my freshman year. Many students mocked her for being so unthinkably old, for looking like a schoolmarm, for loving science, for trembling when she spoke about nature. She would gaze fervently into a beaker as though an entire galaxy spun before her. She grew so excited while recounting the habits of molecules that she would skip about the lab and clap her spotted hands. She would weep for joy over what swam before her in a microscope. Mrs. Givens wept easily, more often than not because of a wisecrack or prank from one of the students. Our cruelty was a defense against the claim she made on us. For she was inviting us to share her passionate curiosity. She called us to hunger and thirst after knowledge of the universe.

I would not join the others in mocking her. I supposed it was pity that held me back, or an ingrained respect for my elders. Only in the fall of my freshman year, on a day when Mrs. Givens brought us here to this field for a botany class, did I realize that I could not mock her because I loved her. She led us through her meadow, naming the plants, twirling the bright fallen leaves, telling which birds ate which berries, opening milkweed pods, disclosing the burrows of groundhogs, parting the weeds to reveal caterpillars and crickets, showing where mice had severed blades of grass. Much of the meadow she had planted, with seeds carried in her pockets from the neighboring countryside. Every few years she burned it, as the Indians had burned the prairies, to keep the woods from reclaiming it.

While Mrs. Givens told us these things in her quavery voice, students kept sidling away to smoke or joke or dabble their hands in the creek, until there were only three of us following her. I stayed with her not from a sense of obedience but from wonder. To know this patch of land, I dimly realized, would be the work of a lifetime. But in knowing it deeply, right down to the foundations, you would comprehend a great deal more, perhaps everything. As she touched the feathery plants of her meadow, as she murmured the names and histories of the creatures who shared the place with her, I came to feel that this was holy ground. And if the meadow was holy, maybe other fields and woods and crossroads and backyards were also holy.

At one point, Mrs. Givens knelt amid the bristly spikes of a tall russet grass. "You see why it's called foxtail, don't you?" she said. "Livestock won't eat it, but you can twist the stalks together and make a fair rope. Farmers used to bind up corn fodder with hanks of foxtail." She grasped one of the spikes, and, with a rake of her thumb, brushed seeds into her palm. She poured a few seeds into my hand and a few into the hands of the other two students who had remained with her. "Now what do you have there?" she asked us.

We stared at the barbed grains in our palms. "Seeds," one of us replied.

"That's the universe unfolding," she told us, "right there in your hands. The same as in every cell of our bodies. Now *why*? That's the question I can't ever get behind. Why should the universe be alive? Why does it obey laws? And why these particular laws? For that matter, why is there a universe at all?" She gave a rollicking laugh. "And isn't it curious that there should be creatures like us who can walk in this beautiful field and puzzle over things?"

She asked her questions gaily, and I have carried them with me all these years in the same spirit. They rose in me again on this October afternoon as I followed the dirt track to the spot where her cottage used to be. Stones marked the cellar hole and the front stoop. Brush grew up through the space left by her death. The woods had reclaimed her meadow. Yet the ground still felt holy. Her marveling gaze had disclosed for me the force and shapeliness of things, and that power survived her passing. She taught me that if only we could be adequate to the given world, we need not dream of paradise.

Reversing my steps, I walked back to the crossroads and kept going west for a hundred yards or so, until I fetched up before the house where, as a simmering teenager, I had wooed a girl. Let me call her Veronica. She and her family moved from Wayland soon after the Army Corps of Engineers built that needless dam, and so on this October day her house was for me another shell filled only with memory. The present kept abrading the past, however, because during the few minutes while I stood there a grown man in a go-cart kept zooming around the yard, following a deeply gouged path. Every time he roared past, he peered at me from beneath his crash helmet. I nodded, assuming the look of one who is infatuated with loud machines and that appeared to satisfy him.

Veronica had the face of a queen on the deck of cards with which I learned to play poker, a face I considered perfect. Words tumbled from her lush lips, impulsively, like rabbits fleeing a burrow. Black wavy hair tumbled down her back, twitching nearly to her slender hips. Having learned in marriage what it means to love a woman, I cannot say that what I felt for Veronica was quite love. Nor was it simply lust, although for much of my seventeenth year the mere thought of her set me aching. At that age, I would have been reluctant to see myself as the urgent stallion and Veronica as the skittish mare.

In her backyard there was a sycamore tree that loomed high over the house, its fat trunk a patchwork of peeling bark and its crooked upper branches as creamy as whole milk. Wooden crossbars nailed to the trunk formed a ladder up to a treehouse. Veronica and I often sat beneath the sycamore on a stone bench, talking and falling silent, aware of parental eyes watching us from the kitchen. With our backs to the house, our sides pressed together, I could risk brushing a hand over her knee, she could run a fingernail under my chin. But even a kiss, our mouths so visibly meeting, would have prompted a visit from the kitchen.

One October day, a day very like this one of my return to Wayland, Veronica and I were sitting on the bench, hunting for words to shape our confusion, when suddenly she leapt to her feet and said, "Let's go up to the treehouse."

"We'll get filthy," I said. I glanced with misgiving at my white knit shirt and chino pants, so carefully pressed. Her lemony blouse was protected by a green corduroy jumper.

"It'll wash out," she said, tugging me by the hand.

I stood. Without waiting for me, she kicked off her shoes and clambered up the wooden rungs, but instead of halting at the rickety platform of the treehouse, she kept on, swaying from limb to limb. I watched until the flashing of her bare legs made me look away.

When she had gone as high as she dared, high enough to escape the view from the kitchen, she balanced on a branch and called to me, "Come on up! Are you afraid?"

I was afraid—but not of the tree. I stepped onto a crossbrace and started climbing, and as I climbed there was nowhere else to look but up, and there was nothing else to see above me except those white legs parted within the green hoop of her skirt. Her creamy forked limbs and the creamy forked limbs of the sycamore merged in my sight, as they merge now in memory, and I was drawn upward into the pale shadows between her thighs. My knowledge of what I was climbing toward would remain abstract for a number of years. I understood only that where her legs joined there was an opening, a gateway for life coming and going. When I reached Veronica I put my hand, briefly, where my gaze had gone, just far enough to feel the surprising warmth of that secret, satiny place. Then I withdrew my hand and she smoothed her skirt, neither of us risking a word, and we teetered there for a hundred heartbeats on those swaying branches, shaken by inner as well as outer winds. Then the kitchen door creaked open and her mother's voice inquired as to our sanity, and we climbed down. I went first, as though to catch Veronica should she fall, my gaze toward the ground.

The buzzing of the go-cart eventually wore through the husk of memory, and my lungs filled with the present. I became again what I was, a man long married, a man with a daughter older than Veronica had been on that day of our climb into the tree. The sycamore still rose behind the house, twenty-five years taller, crisp brown leaves rattling in the wind, the upper limbs as pale and silky as ever.

I had a choice of returning to the church by the road or across the stubble of a cornfield. I chose the field. All the way, I could see the white steepled box gleaming on its rise. The only car in the parking lot was mine. Beyond a treeline to the southwest, beyond the annihilating waters of the reservoir that I could not bear to look at, the sun wallowed down toward dusk. The church might already be locked, I thought, so late on a weekday afternoon. Still I did not hurry. My boots scuffed the ridges where corn had stood. Raccoons and crows would find little to feast on in this stubble, for the harvester had plucked it clean. I recalled the biblical injunction to farmers, that they leave the margins of their fields unpicked, for the poor and the beasts. I thought of the margins in a life, in my life, the untended zones beyond the borders of clarity, the encircling wilderness out of which new powers and visions come.

A cornfield is a good approach to a church, for you arrive with dirt on your boots, the smell of greenery in your nostrils, dust on your tongue. The door would be locked, I figured, and the main door was, the broad entrance through which the Methodist women carried their piety and their pies, through which men carried mortgages and mortality, through which children like myself carried headfuls of questions. But the rear door was unlocked. I left my boots on the stoop and went inside.

The back room I entered had the familiarity of a place one returns to in dream: the squeaky pine boards of the floor, the dwarf tables where children would sit on Sundays to color pictures of Jesus, the brass hooks where the choir would hang their robes and the minister his hat, the folding chairs collapsed into a corner, the asthmatic furnace, and on a counter the stack of lathe-turned walnut plates for the offering.

Every few paces I halted, listening. The joints of the church cricked as the sun let it go. Birds fussed beyond the windows. But no one else was about; this relieved me, for here least of all was I prepared to explain myself. I had moved too long in circles where to confess an interest in religious things marked one as a charlatan, a sentimentalist, or a fool. No doubt I have all three qualities in my character. But I also have another quality, and that is an unshakable hunger to know who I am, where I am, and into what sort of cosmos I have been so briefly and astonishingly sprung. Whatever combination of shady motives might have led me here, the impulse that shook me right then was a craving to glimpse the very source of things.

I made my way out through the choir door into the sanctuary. Cushionless pews in somber ranks, uncarpeted floor, exposed beams in the vault overhead and whitewashed plaster on the walls: it was a room fashioned by men and women who knew barns, for preachers who lived out of saddlebags, in honor of a God who cares nothing for ornament. No tapestries, no shrines, no racks of candles, no gold on the altar, no bragging memorials to vanished patrons. The window glass, unstained, let in the plain light of day.

I sat in a pew midway along the central aisle and looked out through those clear windows. My reasons for coming here were entwined with that sky full of light. As a boy I had looked out, Sunday after Sunday, to see corn grow and clouds blow, to watch crows bustle among the tops of trees, to follow hawks, unmindful of the Sabbath, on their spiraling hunts, and to sense in all this radiant surge the same rush I felt under my fingers when I pressed a hand to my throat. There was no gulf between outside and inside. We gathered in this room not to withdraw, but more fully to enter the world.

On this day of my return I kept watching the sky as the light thinned and the darkness thickened. I became afraid. Afraid of dying, yes, but even more of not having lived, afraid of passing my days in a stupor, afraid of squandering my moment in the light. I gripped the pew in front of me to still my trembling. I wanted to dive down to the center of being, touch bedrock, open my eyes and truly, finally, unmistakably see. I shifted my gaze from the darkening window to the altar, to the wooden cross, to the black lip of the Bible showing from the pulpit. But those were only props for a play that was forever in rehearsal, the actors clumsy, the script obscure. I was myself one of the actors, sustained in my bumbling efforts by the hope that one day the performance would be perfect, and everything would at last come clear.

One cannot summon grace with a whistle. The pew beneath me, the air around me, the darkening windows did not turn to fire. The clouds of unknowing did not part. I sat there for a long while, and then I rose and made my way down the aisle, past the organ, through the choir door and back room, out into the freshening night. On the stoop I drew on my boots and laced them up. The chrome latch of my car was already cool. I drove back through the crossroads with headlights glaring, alert for animals that might dash before me in the confusion of dusk.

There is more to be seen at any crossroads than one can see in a lifetime of looking. My return visit to Wayland was less than two hours long. Once again several hundred miles distant from that place, back here in my home ground making this model from slippery words, I cannot be sure where the pressure of mind has warped the surface of things. If you were to go there, you would not find every detail exactly as I have described it. How could you, bearing as you do a past quite different from mine? No doubt my memory, welling up through these lines, has played tricks with time and space.

What memory is made of I cannot say; my body, at least, is made of atoms on loan from the earth. How implausible, that these atoms should have gathered to form this *I*, this envelope of skin that walks about and strokes horses and tastes apples and trembles with desire in the branches of a sycamore and gazes through the windows of a church at the ordinary sky. Certain moments in one's life cast their influence forward over all the moments that follow. My encounters in Wayland shaped me first as I lived through them, then again as I recalled them during my visit, and now as I write them down. That is of course why I write them down. The self is a fiction. I make up the story of myself with scraps of memory, sensation, reading, and hearsay. It is a tale I whisper against the dark. Only in rare moments of luck or courage do I hush, forget myself entirely, and listen to the silence that precedes and surrounds and follows all speech.

If you have been keeping count, you may have toted up seven mysteries, or maybe seven times seven, or maybe seven to the seventh power. My hunch is that, however we count, there is only one mystery. In our nearsightedness, we merely glimpse the light scintillating off the numberless scales of Leviathan, and we take each spark for a separate wonder.

Could we bear to see all the light at once? Could we bear the roar of infinite silence? I sympathize with science, where, in order to answer a question, you limit the variables. You draw a circle within which everything can be measured, and you shut out the rest of the universe. I draw my own circles with these narratives, telling of rivers and tornadoes, house and family, dirt and dreams. I lay out stories like fences to enclose for myself a home ground within the frightening infinities. Yet every enclosure is a makeshift, every boundary an illusion. With great ingenuity, we decipher some of the rules that govern this vast shining dance, but all our efforts could not change the least of them.

Nothing less than the undivided universe can be our true home. Yet how can one speak or even think about the whole of things? Language is of only modest help. Every sentence is a wispy net, capturing a few flecks of meaning. The sun shines without vocabulary. The salmon has no name for the urge that drives it upstream. The newborn groping for the nipple knows hunger long before it knows a single word. Even with an entire dictionary in one's head, one eventually comes to the end of words. Then what? Then drink deep like the baby, swim like the salmon, burn like any brief star.

N O T E S

I am not a scholar, as you will have noticed, but I am a reader. I agree with Gary Snyder that "in this huge old occidental culture our teaching elders are books. *Books are our grandparents!*" [*The Practice of the Wild* (San Francisco: North Point, 1990), p. 61]. I didn't want to lumber up my pages with notes—as I lumbered up the preceding sentence—or to compile bibliographies, for that would have given a false appearance of expertise; but I do want to acknowledge some of my elders, the books that are my grandparents. So I will list here briefly the sources from which I quote, and at least a few of the sources from which I have learned.

2

HOUSE AND HOME

20   Out of gratitude and affection, I want to mention here that my favorite resource for singing children to sleep, *The Folk Songs of North America* (Garden City, New York: Doubleday, 1960), was compiled by Alan Lomax,

son of the great collector of American songs, John A. Lomax.

24   Thoreau devotes a section of *Walden* to "Shelter." The remark I quote comes from the J. Lyndon Shanley edition (Princeton: Princeton UP, 1973), p. 46.

31   "The Death of the Hired Man" appears in *Complete Poems of Robert Frost* (New York: Holt, Rinehart and Winston, 1964), this passage on p. 53.

34   "The Design of a House" is in Wendell Berry's *Collected Poems 1957–1982* (San Francisco: North Point, 1985), p. 29.

3

EARTH'S BODY

45   I learned about *Chipko* from Barry Greer's profile of Dr. Vandana Shiva, "Putting Science In Its Place," *What's Happening* (29 November 1990), pp. 1, 4–5.

46   I quote Walt Whitman from section 6 of *Song of Myself*, in *Leaves of Grass*, ed. Sculley Bradley and Harold W. Blodgett (New York: Norton, 1973), pp. 33–35.

47   Browning's lyric comes from "Pippa Passes," *Poems of Robert Browning* (London: Oxford UP, 1907), p. 171.

55   "Living midnight": *The Secret of the Golden Flower*, trans. Thomas Cleary (San Francisco: Harper, 1991), pp. 42, 59–60.

4

THE FORCE OF MOVING WATER

63   Mark Twain, *Life on the Mississippi* [1883], in *Mississippi Writings*, ed. Guy Cardwell (New York: Library of America, 1982), p. 245.

65–66   Zadok Cramer, *The Navigator*, 8th ed. (Pittsburgh: Cramer, Spear and Eichbaum, 1814; reprint: Readex Microprint, 1966), p. 246.

66–67   Alexander Wilson's words on Big Bone Lick are quoted by Joseph Kastner in *A Species of Eternity* (New York: Dutton, 1978), p. 177.

70   Charles Dickens recounted his meeting with the Choctaw chief in *American Notes for General Circulation* [1842] (reprinted Gloucester, Mass.: Peter Smith, 1968), pp. 191–93.

70   The "blood thirsty" lyrics are quoted in Richard E. Banta, *The Ohio* (New York: Rinehart, 1949), pp. 266–67.

74   "Colonel Christopher Gist's Journal" appears in *First Explorations of Kentucky*, ed. J. Stoddard Johnston, Filson Club Publications No. 13 (Louisville: Morton, 1898), pp. 101–85. I quote from p. 133.

74–75   George Washington's journal: "Washington's Tour to the Ohio," *Old South Leaflets*, no. 41 (1893), pp. 1–12. Washington's newspaper advertisement is reproduced in *The Ohio River Handbook and Picture Album*, ed. Benjamin F. Klein (Cincinnati: Young and Klein, 1969), p. 67.

76   Manasseh Cutler, "Description of Ohio" [1787], *Old South Leaflets*, no. 40 (1892), pp. 10–11.

76–77   George Croghan, *A Selection of Letters and Journals Relating to Tours into the Western Country* [1750–1765], in *Early Western Travels 1748–1846*, ed. Reuben Gold Thwaites (Cleveland: Clark, 1904), vol. 1, pp. 131–32.

77   John James Audubon, "The Ohio," in *Audubon and His Journals*, ed. Maria Audubon (New York: Scribner's, 1897), vol. 2, pp. 205–6.

77   The swimming bear was reported by John Woods in *Two Years' Residence on the English Prairie of Illinois* [1822], ed. Paul M. Angle (Chicago: Lakeside Press, 1968), p. 93.

78   Audubon told about the giant catfish in "Fishing in the Ohio," in *Audubon and His Journals*, vol. 2, p. 215.

79   Francis Parkman offered his description of the frontier in *France and England in North America* [1851–1892] (New York: Library of America, 1983), vol. 2, pp. 1073–74.

80   The garden of Eden song is quoted in Banta, *The Ohio*, pp. 266–67.

80–81   Audubon: "Passenger Pigeon," originally in *Ornitholog-*

ical Biography [1831–39], reprinted in *Audubon Reader*, ed. Scott Russell Sanders (Bloomington: Indiana UP, 1986), pp. 116–23.

81 Cramer on cane: *The Navigator*, p. 127.

83 President Hoover's words are quoted in *The Ohio River Handbook*, p. 373.

84 The tourist who celebrated "the buzz of employment" was Thaddeus Harris, author of *Journal of a Tour into the Territory Northwest of the Alleghany Mountains; Made in the Spring of the Year 1803* (Boston: Manning and Loring, 1805); these words come from p. 51.

85 The minister willing "to cut down all the trees in the universe" was James Dixon, who reported his sentiments in *Methodism in America* (London: Printed for the Author, 1849), p. 104.

85 The Kentucky Congressman is quoted in Archer Butler Hulbert, *The Ohio River: A Course of Empire* (New York: Putnam's, 1906), p. 359.

86 Beauty of the Ohio River: Thomas Hutchins, *Journal from Fort Pitt to the Mouth of the Ohio in the Year 1766* in *Oyo: An Ohio River Anthology*, ed. Don Wallis (Yellow Springs, Ohio: OYO Press, 1988), vol. 2, p. 21; Thomas Jefferson, *Notes on the State of Virginia* [1784–85], ed. Thomas Perkins Abernethy (New York: Harper and Row, 1964), p. 8; Cramer, *The Navigator*, p. 24.

86 Frances Trollope voiced her desire for "the romance of real life" in *Domestic Manners of the Americans* [1832] (New York: Dodd, Mead, 1901), vol. 1, p. 46.

86 Dickens, *American Notes*, p. 185.

87 The German traveler was Moritz Busch, whose impressions have been published in *Travels between the Hudson and the Mississippi 1851–1852*, trans. and ed. Norman H. Binger (Lexington: UP of Kentucky, 1971); this passage comes from p. 206.

87 The nuisance of old trees: Washington, "Washington's Tour to the Ohio," p. 8; Trollope, *Domestic Manners of the Americans*, vol. 1, p. 59.

87–88 American observers on the Ohio: Charles Fenno Hoffman, *A Winter in the West* (New York: Harper and Brothers, 1835), vol. 1, pp. 49–50, 57; Walt Whitman, *The Uncollected Poetry and Prose of Walt Whitman*, ed. Emory Holloway (Garden City, New York: Doubleday, 1921), vol. 1, p. 187.

88–89   Audubon's reflections on changes in the river country appear in "The Ohio," *Audubon and His Journals*, vol. 2, pp. 206–7.

90   Theodore Roethke on water: *Straw for the Fire: From the Notebooks of Theodore Roethke 1943–1963*, ed. David Wagoner (Garden City, New York: Anchor, 1974), p. 96.

5

SETTLING DOWN

103   John Berryman died in 1972. These lines appear in "Roots," from the posthumous volume, *Henry's Fate & Other Poems 1967–1972* (New York: Farrar, Straus and Giroux, 1977), p. 58.

103–6   Salman Rushdie, *Imaginary Homelands: Essays and Criticism 1981–1991* (New York: Viking, 1991), pp. 124–5, 394, 124, 125.

108–10   My several quotations from Bruce Chatwin's *The Songlines* (New York: Viking, 1987) come, in order, from pp. 161, 227, 13, and 178; the single quotation from *What Am I Doing Here* (New York: Viking, 1989) is from pp. 221–22.

110–11   Gary Snyder, *The Old Ways* (San Francisco: City Lights, 1977), p. 59.

112   Aldo Leopold, *A Sand County Almanac* [1949] (New York: Ballantine, 1970), pp. 262, 210.

112   Gilbert White's *The Natural History and Antiquities of Selborne* was published in 1789. I quote from a modern edition compiled by Ronald Davidson-Houston, *The Illustrated Natural History of Selborne* (New York: St. Martin's, 1981), p. 15.

113   Gary Snyder, *The Real Work: Interviews and Talks 1964–1979* (New York: New Directions, 1980), p. 117.

115   Thich Nhat Hanh, *The Miracle of Mindfulness*, revised ed.
       (Boston: Beacon, 1987), p. 36.

116   René Dubos, *The Wooing of Earth* (New York: Scribner's,
       1980), pp. 5, 50.

116   Wendell Berry, *Standing by Words* (San Francisco: North
       Point, 1983), p. 111.

120   Thoreau's caution appears in his journal for November
       20, 1857. I quote from *H. D. Thoreau: A Writer's Journal*,
       ed. Laurence Stapleton (New York: Dover, 1960), p. 173.

6

GROUND NOTES

129   Thoreau's promise of a "solid bottom" comes from the
       last chapter of *Walden* (1854). Again I quote from the
       Shanley edition, p. 330. The passage about digging down
       to reality is from the second chapter, "Where I Lived and
       What I Lived For," pp. 97–98.

129   The English spelling of Lao-tzu's name and the transla-
       tion of the title of the book attributed to him, *Tao Te
       Ching*, vary from one authority to another. I quote him
       here from *The Wisdom of Laotse*, ed. and trans. Lin Yu-
       tang (New York: The Modern Library, 1948), p. 64.

130   I quote *The Upanishads* from a selection translated by Al-
       istair Shearer and Peter Russell (New York: Harper &
       Row, 1978), p. 26.

130–31 *The Wisdom of Laotse*, p. 145.

133   Werner Heisenberg discusses the implications of the un-
       certainty principle, and of quantum theory generally, in
       Physics and Philosophy: The Revolution in Modern Science
       (New York: Harper & Brothers, 1958). I quote from p.
       58.

134   *Walden*, p. 330.

134   Again I quote from the Davidson-Houston edition of
       Gilbert White, *The Illustrated Natural History of Selborne*,
       p. 181.

135   "The Whiteness of the Whale" is chapter 42 in *Moby-*

Dick (1851). I draw on the text edited by Harrison Hayford and Hershel Parker (New York: Norton, 1967), p. 169.

136 Steven Weinberg: *The First Three Minutes: A Modern View of the Origin of the Universe* (New York: Basic Books, 1977), p. 154.

136 James Peebles is quoted in Alan Lightman and Roberta Brawer's *Origins: The Lives and Worlds of Modern Cosmologists* (Cambridge: Harvard UP, 1990), p. 231. Lightman and Brawer ask all but one of their twenty-seven interviewees to respond to the Weinberg quotation.

137 Thomas Berry, *The Dream of the Earth* (San Francisco: Sierra Club Books, 1988), p. 24.

139 Thoreau's sentence about wildness appears in "Walking," first published in 1862. I quote from *Thoreau: The Major Essays*, ed. Jeffrey L. Duncan (New York: Dutton, 1972), p. 209.

139 Gary Snyder, *The Practice of the Wild* (San Francisco: North Point, 1990), p. 103.

140 Berry, *The Dream of the Earth*, pp. 38–39.

7

TELLING THE HOLY

146 I call my visionary neighbor "Jeremiah Lofts" because that is the name I gave him in a short story entitled "Prophet," which appeared in my book *Fetching the Dead* ([Urbana: U of Illinois P, 1984], pp. 96–110). The account I give here is closer than "Prophet" to the actual events as I remember them.

151 The remarks by E. M. Forster come from his chapter on "The Story" in *Aspects of the Novel* (London: Arnold, 1927), pp. 27, 41.

152 "The Terror of History" is the title of chapter four in Mircea Eliade's *Cosmos and History: The Myth of the Eternal Return* (New York: Harper, 1959). The passage about primitive cultures appears on p. 90.

153   Joseph Campbell on myth: *The Hero with a Thousand Faces*, 2d ed. (Princeton: Princeton UP, 1968), pp. 257–58.

153   I quote "The American Scholar" [1837] from *Ralph Waldo Emerson: Essays & Lectures*, ed. Joel Porte (New York: Library of America, 1983), p. 55.

154   Apache word for myth: Keith H. Basso, "Stalking with Stories," in *On Nature*, ed. Daniel Halpern (San Francisco: North Point, 1986), p. 103.

155   Peter Matthiessen, *The Snow Leopard* (New York: Viking, 1978), p. 40.

155–56 Barry Lopez, *Arctic Dreams: Imagination and Desire in a Northern Landscape* (New York: Charles Scribner's Sons, 1986), p. 297.

156   Gary Snyder on "primitive": *The Real Work*, p. 115.

157   Flannery O'Connor on being a storyteller: *Mystery and Manners*, ed. Sally and Robert Fitzgerald (New York: Farrar, Straus and Giroux, 1962), p. 192.

158   James Gunn is quoted in Lightman and Brawer's *Origins*, p. 258.

158   Emerson's grand sentence about sentences appears in his journal for 19 December 1834. I quote from *The Heart of Emerson's Journal*, ed. Bliss Perry (Boston: Houghton Mifflin, 1914), p. 89.

159   Chuang Tzu's warning is translated by Thomas Merton in *The Way of Chuang Tzu* (New York: New Directions, 1965), p. 130.

159   The remark by Edwin Turner comes from Lightman and Brawer's *Origins*, p. 322.

160   Flannery O'Connor's letters were edited and collected by Sally Fitzgerald in *The Habit of Being* (New York: Vintage, 1980). O'Connor speaks about the Holy in a letter to John Hawkes, on 13 September 1959 (p. 349).

160–61 Reynolds Price, *A Palpable God* (San Francisco: North Point, 1985), pp. 34, 46.

162   Charles Misner's statement also comes from Lightman and Brawer's invaluable collection of interviews, *Origins*, p. 247.

163 The Apache storyteller is quoted by Campbell in *The Hero with a Thousand Faces*, p. 169.

165 Thomas Merton wrote about paradise to the great Zen master, Daisetz T. Suzuki, in a letter of 30 November 1959, which appears in *The Hidden Ground of Love: The Letters of Thomas Merton on Religious Experience and Social Concerns*, ed. William H. Shannon (New York: Farrar, Straus and Giroux, 1985), p. 571.

166 O'Connor, *Mystery and Manners*, p. 192.

169 Chatwin, *The Songlines*, p. 52.